TRAGIC
DECEPTION

OTHER BOOKS
BY HAMILTON FISH

The Challenge of World Communism

The Red Plotters

*An American Manifesto of Freedom in
    Answer to the Manifesto on
    Communism (1848)*

*The American People Are Living on Top
    of a Nuclear Volcano*

FDR: The Other Side of the Coin

*Lafayette in America During and After
    the Revolutionary War*

*New York State: The Battleground of the
    Revolutionary War*

TRAGIC DECEPTION

FDR AND AMERICA'S INVOLVEMENT IN WORLD WAR II

by

HAMILTON FISH

Devin-Adair, Publishers
Old Greenwich, Connecticut

Library of Congress Cataloging in Publication Data

Fish, Hamilton, 1888-
  Tragic Deception.

  1. World War, 1939-1945 — United States. 2. United States — Foreign
relations — 1933-1945. 3. United States — Politics and government —1933-
1945. 4. Roosevelt, Franklin D. (Franklin Delano), 1882-1945.
I. Title.
D742.U5F57 1983   940.53'73   82-19876
ISBN 0-8159-6917-1

DEDICATION

This book is dedicated to:

Pope John Paul II, the greatest fighter for maintenance of freedom of religion;

Alexander Solzhenitsyn, the greatest freedom fighter in the world;

Andrei Sakharov, another great freedom fighter;

Twenty million American veterans who fought for freedom and democracy in four wars;

And above all, to the preservation of freedom in the United States and throughout the world.

CONTENTS

Preface xiii

Introduction 3

I. How the United States Became Involved in
World War II 13

II. The Tragedy of Pearl Harbor 22

III. How Roosevelt Prodded the British
Government into War 42

IV. "Your Boys Are Not Going To Be Sent into
Any Foreign Wars" 46

V. The March to War 55

VI. Interview With the German Foreign Minister, Joachim von Ribbentrop, August 14,
1939 69

VII. Peaceful Arbitration or War? 83

VIII. The Jewish Question 97

Conclusion 102

Appendix 103

Addendum 111

ILLUSTRATIONS

1. Hamilton Fish at eight years old: 1895

2. Hamilton Fish: All-American tackle from Harvard: 1910.

3. Hamilton Fish with his troops in World War I.

4. Major Hamilton Fish of the 369th Negro infantry: 1919.

5. Hamilton Fish as candidate running for the New York State Assembly on the Progressive ("Bull Moose") ticket

6. U.S. Congressman from New York: 1920-45

7. Brochure supporting Hamilton Fish for President: 1935.

8. With General Douglas MacArthur: 1962

9. Hamilton Fish, President Dwight Eisenhower, Honorable Clare Boothe Luce, General Mark Clark, and former Ambassador to Switzerland, Henry J. Taylor: 1964.

10. Past National Commander of the American Legion.

11. Hamilton Fish today.

Devin-Adair, Publishers is America's foremost publisher of quality conservative books. Founded in 1911, the company has championed the cause of the Thinking Right, and historically has published the work of major conservative writers. In recent years, Devin-Adair has increased its emphasis in this area and today is considered the leading publishing firm on the right.

The firm also has a long-standing reputation for works of significance in the fields of ecology, Irish literature, health, and nutrition. It publishes superbly illustrated nature and travel books on the Eastern seaboard through its Chatham Press subsidiary.

Devin-Adair's newest emphasis is in the area of books, programs, and software relating to the personal computer.

Devin-Adair operates the Veritas Book Club for conservative readers, the Ecological Book Club for nature and health audiences, and the Irish-American Book Society.

Publisher: C. de la Belle Issue
Managing Director: Roger H. Lourie
Cover Design: Debra Fram
Production: Arthur Hamparian

Devin-Adair, Publishers
143 Sound Beach Avenue
P.O. Box A
Old Greenwich, CT 06870

EXCELLENCE, SINCE 1911

PREFACE

Hamilton Fish. It is a name that evokes dim memories of another age, of a time when, it seemed to us as children, great issues were debated and decided upon by great men. It was an epoch peopled by giants, and giants they remain today, remembered by history, mostly, because few are left.

Hamilton Fish: friend and foe of presidents, historian, author, statesman, outspoken American freedom-fighter, is one who remains. He is as venerable as the great trees that benignly guard his estate in Newburgh, New York. Yet in heart and mind he is very much of the present, concerned lest the tragic events of more than 40 years ago, when an American president, besotted with power and in the grip of Messianic delusions, manipulated his country into a war of horrific dimensions, a war that permitted an Iron Curtain to drop with the clang of finality over Eastern Europe, and that ultimately created the paranoiac nuclear miasma that beclouds the world today.

Hamilton Fish never was, and is not now, though he has lived for 94 years, a mere observer of history. In this century he has immersed himself in the tides of national and international events. At the threshold of the war that was to change the course of history forever, he stood athwart the imperalistic winds emanating from Washington and dared to cry halt.

And today, from the special vantage point conferred by his years and his experience and his wisdom, he continues to cry halt: halt to assaults on the U.S. Constitution by government power-brokers and a wrong-headed judiciary; halt to the one-worlders who control international affairs through powerful financial institutions; and halt, most fervently, to the relentless forces of communism that sweep before them nation after nation, continent after continent, in pursuit of the ultimate goal.

From where does such a force spring? And why, in the twilight of our century, do such men stand so heroically, seemingly alone in outspoken courage? Forty years is not, after all, so long ago. Have we, as a nation and a people, changed so much since then that a man of Hamilton Fish's calibre becomes, indeed, a rarity?

He is a man of stature. Physically, he stands above us all, and his eyes pierce with the passion of his commitment. His voice is stentorian, overlaid with the aristocratic, upper-Hudson inflections made familiar to the American public by Fish's one-time friend and mentor, Franklin Roosevelt. His memory is awesome, the more so as it encompasses nearly a century of events, great and small.

With the exception of Woodrow Wilson, he has known every 20th-century president, beginning with Theodore Roosevelt. And one senses, in talking with Fish, that TR is the president he admires most. He numbers him, with Patrick Henry and Abraham Lincoln, as the philosophers and statesmen from whom his own philsophy was formed.

But to appreciate Hamilton Fish (an inadequate evaluation, that: as one learns to know him, it is more appropriate to say, as one increasingly comes to *esteem* him), and to decipher the ethos of a man whose devotion has remained steadfast for over 70 years, it is significant to explore the roots from whence he came.

The name "Hamilton," which generations of Fishes have borne, derives from Alexander Hamilton, the closest friend of Nicholas Fish (1758-1833), a prominent figure in the Revolutionary War and an ardent Federalist. At 18, Nicholas Fish became the youngest major ever commissioned by the Continental Congress — by an order signed by John Hancock.

Though an intimate of Alexander Hamilton, Fish refused his request to second him in his dual with Burr, forseeing, perhaps, the tragic outcome.

Nicholas Fish was also a close friend of the Marquis de Lafayette. Today the Fish family retains over 40 letters from Lafayette to Nicholas Fish, in addition to at least one communication *about* the Marquis. DeWitt Clinton, Governor of New York, wrote to Fish: "... tell Lafayette that the people of New York state, who are very religious, wonder why he does not go to church on Sunday."

The first Hamilton Fish (1808-93), the son of Nicholas and named for Alexander Hamilton, was heir to the Federalist tradition and gravitated naturally to politics as a Whig. A U.S. Representative (1843-45), he was elected lieutenant governor of New York in 1847 and governor for a two-year term in 1848. He served as U.S. Senator from 1851 to 1857. He was a moderate anti-slavery man who opposed extremism among both abolitionist and pro-slavery factions. He deplored the breakup of the Whigs as a national party, and spent a decade away from national politics, devoting himself to private and civil affairs in New York City.

But Fish was one of the many to lionize the victorious Civil War general Ulysses S. Grant, and in 1869 he was appointed Grant's secretary of state. He was in the cabinet longer than any other member and is considered one of the ablest secretaries of state in U.S. history. His greatest achievement as Secretary was bringing about the Treaty of Washington, which paved the way for settlement of the Alabama Claims and other longstanding disputes with Great Britain. After he left office in 1877, Fish resumed his labors for Columbia College, of which he had long been chairman of the board of trustees, and he was largely responsible for the emergence of Columbia as a true university.

This first Hamilton Fish's three sons distinguished themselves in varied and multiple endeavors. Nicholas (1848-1902) entered the diplomatic sevice and was minister to Belgium from 1882 to 1886. Stuyvesant (1851-1923) became a director of the Illinois Central Railroad in 1877, and as its president from 1887 to 1907, he built the railroad into a large system. A third son, Hamilton (1849-1936), was a member of the New York state assembly (1884-96) serving as speaker in 1895-96, and was for many years Republican boss of Putnam County, New York. Upon appointment by President Theodore Roosevelt, he was Assistant Treasurer of the United States in New York City and also served one term as U.S. representative.

From such a heritage did the author of this book evolve: a family inured in the warp of the American tapestry; lives dedicated to, toughened by, and intricately a part of United States political and social history. It is no wonder that Hamilton Fish, coming of age on the eve of the first Great War, and coming from a line of statesmen whose very essence was bound up in political America, was to play such a crucial role as his friend, Franklin Roosevelt, moved the country inexorably toward the second. And it is no surprise that today, at 94, Hamilton Fish is compelled to warn the nation, whose heritage is his own, of the tragic consequences of political power run amok. Fish knows. He has been there.

At Harvard, where he took his undergraduate degree, Hamilton Fish, in another great national tradition, was an outstanding and famous football star, named to the all-time All American Team in 1910. While Fish was achieving fame as a tackle with a charge "like the recoil of a steel spring," another young American, who was to acquire celebrity of a very different sort, was rooting Harvard to victory as a cheerleader. Fish remembers John (Jack) Reed, the poet/journalist who became the author of *Ten Days That Shook The World*, the pro-Marxist account of the Russian Revolution, as an idealist, a socialist without guile or sinister motive. Today, Fish believes that the Bolsheviks "poisoned Reed, trapped him for propaganda purposes."

It was in these undergraduate years that Teddy Roosevelt became, perhaps, Fish's first role model (not to discount the legacy of his own family), and his awe of TR has not diminished with the passage of time.

Roosevelt was acquainted with Fish's father, and Hamilton and TR's son attended Harvard together, belonged to the Porcellian together, and Fish served as best man at young Roosevelt's wedding. When, as was perhaps inevitable, Fish came to politics, he ran on TR's Progressive (Bull Moose) ticket and was elected three times to the New York state assembly.

It was also in these years — in 1913-1914 — that another Roosevelt moved into Hamilton Fish's life. Fish remembers FDR then as "goodlooking, intelligent, funny." He was, in Fish's terms, a "good American," who believed in the Constitution and in private enterprise. He was in "no way radical or socialistic in those days."

They were friendly, and mutually supportive (Roosevelt wanted Fish to succeed him in the New York state senate) for 20 years. They shared the same views. Both were forward-looking, Jeffersonian in their vision for America. At the end, in 1945, Roosevelt, sick and dying, had only bitterness and hatred for his one-time friend and protege.

Why? What happened to change so dramatically a

relationship forged in common bonds of geography, background, and political and social ideology?

The reasons are straightforward enough, and may be found in what today Hamilton Fish describes as his greatest achievement as a Congressman:

> . . . as ranking Republican member of the Foreign Affairs and Rules Committees, I led the fight in the House of Representatives for three years against FDR's determination not only to get England and France into war against Hitler, but to get [the U.S.] into the war as soon as it started in '39.

And in addition, in what he says was his greatest *failure* in Congress:

> . . . to prevent the outbreak of World War II as Chairman of the Congressional Interparliamentary Union [a bipartisan committee of 20 congressman and four senators]. . . . I introduced a moratorium of 30 days to solve the Danzig war issue by arbitration and peaceful mediation by England, France, Germany, and Italy. I made by far the most important and effective speech to the 300 members of the 30 different nations at Oslo, two weeks before the war, urging the adoption of that resolution in order to prevent the outbreak of World War II.
>
> I pointed out that that was the main function of every delegate — to try and prevent what would be the most disastrous war in history. . . . I pointed out that the peace-making apparatus had broken down and that unless we acted, which was our paramount

function, the war would break out within ten days to two weeks . . .

My speech was the greatest I ever made because it came from my mind, my heart, and my soul. I received a standing ovation for a considerable time. Evidently, when the news reached Roosevelt and Churchill, they were able to persuade the British delegation to oppose [the resolution]. I made it clear that if any of the four participants refused to support my resolution, I would withdraw it.

It really was a terrible tragedy because [I] came so very near to getting that resolution through. . . . If the Danzig issue had been settled peacefully, Hitler and Stalin would have fought it out, to the applause of the free world, hoping each would destroy the other.

These events, then, constituted a complete break with Roosevelt; caused, Fish maintains, by the radical change in FDR himself. Fish analyzes Roosevelt's evolution as "Jeffersonian democrat to left wing democrat to radical democrat to socialist to pro-communist."

Fish has had the benefit of many years to so analyze the radical changes in a man who has been virtually mythologized by the American press and public. He is convinced that FDR began to veer from his Jeffersonian philosophy during his service in Woodrow Wilson's administration, absorbing Wilson's internationalist interventionist policies and incorporating them into his own world view, which would come to fruition in his third presidential term.

Hamilton Fish seems harsh and unrelenting in his

judgment of Roosevelt today. He has written this book with the objective of driving home to the American people the dire results occasioned by the **usurpation of constitutional and congressional** power by an imperialistic president. This warning comes directly from his personal experience with Roosevelt, seen in retrospect, of course, but issuing from the current international climate, perceived by Fish (amongst many others) as fraught with dangers even more insidious than those caused by the United States' entrance into World War II.

What Roosevelt became by 1940, Fish believes, resulted from "a lust for power [which he] wanted to maintain. . . . [he] thought he was bigger than Congress, his party, the Constitution . . . [he believed] he could do anything he wanted."

Fish maintains that when FDR came to Washington, he brought with him a "host of young radicals to create a welfare state . . . [he] catered to the extreme radicals in the labor organizations [especially] the pro-communist CIO." Fish believes that Roosevelt was influenced by Henry Wallace — "a communist all the time . . . a radical as secretary of agriculture (who) brought in Tugwell and other communists, including Alger Hiss . . ."

Fish's judgment of FDR is the judgment of hindsight, reinforced by documented revisionist history. But in 1938, Fish knew, most crucially, only that his one-time friend, the leader of his beloved country, had somehow radically changed and was moving the nation into a war that would have not only devastating immediate results in terms of lives lost and billions spent, but far-reaching ramifications in the years following. And, as is all too evident today, Fish's prescience after the Yalta giveaway has been borne out.

Hamilton Fish was, and is, anti-war. (Who, one may logically ask, is pro-war? Those, as the liberals would have us believe, who urge a powerful national defense today? Ironically, Fish numbers himself among the supporters of President Reagan's defense policies.) Yet in 1917, he went to war. As an officer in the 369th Negro infantry, he served with such distinction that he won the Silver Star and the French Croix de Guerre. And in 1919, as a district commander of the American Legion, he was appointed chairman of the Committee of Three to write the preamble to the Legion's constitution.

He is (justifiably) proud of this document, which has been called "forward-looking and dynamic," and which Presidents Truman and Eisenhower numbered ". . . among the greatest American documents." Fish and his committee dedicated the preamble to God and country which, along with peace and freedom, he considers the four greatest words in any language. "They create a creed everybody can agree with," he says.

In 1920 Hamilton Fish ran for Congress as a Republican and was elected in the GOP landslide. He choose positions on the Foreign Affairs and Banking Committees. Fish's reminiscences of those years as a young Congressman are highlighted by moments of poignant significance:

- In 1921, he introduced his first bill: to bring back the body of an unknown American soldier for burial in the amphitheater in Washington. The bill was the last signed by President Woodrow Wilson, on March 4, 1921. On November 11, 1921, the War Department authorized Fish to place the only wreath on the grave, which represented all American armed forces.
- Fish had served with Negro troops in the war. He came to a Congress in which there where no black representatives. And there he fought bitter battles with Southern Democrats — for black civil rights, for equal treatment with whites, for an anti-lynching law, for a battle monument dedicated to black troops.
- In 1922, Fish put through a "Palestine Resolution," promoting a homeland for the Jews. (He calls it the "American Balfour Resolution.") Through "careful wording [and with] the great orator Burt Cochran to back me up [it was] manipulated through the Foreign Affairs Committee.... The President signed and it became law."
- He introduced a bill providing $10 million in aid to the "starving Germans," who "otherwise would go communist." Again, it was a resolution needing a big fight to ensure passage.
- Fish never thought much of Warren Harding, whom he lists as one of the nation's worst presidents. Though a Republican, Fish maintains "corruption is corruption, no matter who is the cause of it." But he greatly admired Calvin Coolidge, with whom he was very friendly.

• In 1932, as Herbert Hoover was attempting to get reelected, Fish was asked to deliver the keynote speech on his behalf at the Republican state convention at Buffalo, New York. In the speech, which got an enthusiastic reception, and which Fish believes brought him to the attention of national leaders, Fish had originally included a referendum in favor of permitting the use of "light wine and beer." (This was during Prohibition, recall.) When he was shown the speech, however, Hoover insisted that the referendum be deleted in deference to his wife, Lou, a "white-ribboner, a 100 percent out-and-out prohibitioner."

Fish assesses Herbert Hoover as "a fine man, [but] poor politician [who] meant to be a good president."

Hamilton Fish and Herbert Hoover did agree in one essential: opposition to America's entrance into World War II. As war clouds massed over Europe, and Fish recognized FDR's intentions to maneuver the U.S. into the struggle, he rose up to speak, with the considerable force and influence he then commanded, against U.S. intervention into what he and a majority of Americans, in and out of Congress, considered a European affair.

Fish was against our entrance into the war because he is, through and through, a non-interventionist. He is not, however, by his own definition, an isolationist, as he was so called at the time:

> I would certainly not describe myself as an isolationist. The word "isolationist" was a complete misnomer, used by the pro-war interventionists back in the 1930s and '40s to stigmatize those Americans,

representing 85 percent of the country, who were
non-interventionists (unless the U.S. were attacked).

I knew only one isolationist, and that was George
Tinkham, a Republican congressman from Boston,
who was even opposed to making agreements or
treaties, and believed honestly and sincerely in
almost complete isolation.

Virtually all of the American people came to this
country from foreign lands in order to escape either
religious or governmental oppression, and naturally
did not want to become involved in the ancient blood
feuds of foreign nations.

And that is why, prior to World War II, we
opposed joining in the battles fought for domination
in Europe.

Yet, like all Americans, Fish was outraged when
Japan attacked Pearl Harbor. His speech on December
8, 1941, the first ever broadcast from Congress,
gave complete support to President Roosevelt's
"Day of Infamy" declaration. Today, sadly, he says:
"Now I have to repudiate everything I said [then],
because no member of Congress at that time knew
Roosevelt had served a war ultimatum on Japan ten
days before Pearl Harbor." Because he now knows of
what he considers Roosevelt's betrayal, his maneuvering and manipulation of an innocent and unsuspecting American citizenry, Hamilton Fish has written this book.

How will the public view this castigation, this
repudiation of Franklin Roosevelt? One senses in
Fish's judgment of FDR not so much a judgment of
the man (as who but God can judge?) but rage at his

betrayal of America. Fish believed always, and continues to do so today, that the U.S. *must* defend itself if attacked. And in 1941, the country was, indeed, attacked by outside forces. Now, of course, Fish is convinced that this attack was cynically engineered by a president driven by imperialist motives, determined that the United States should become involved in a war not of our making, that did not concern us, that certainly should not be waged at the expense of American lives.

Hamilton Fish holds true to this ideal: that wars should be fought only defensively: in defense of freedom, in defense of unalienable rights, in defense of *one's own people and property.* It is not a tenet with which he necessarily expects agreement; he knows there is legitimate (and patriotic) basis for a differing view.

(It is significant that in 1954 he testified to the Senate that any American military involvement in Southeast Asia would lead the U.S. into a land jungle war in Asia. He testified that it would be a long war, costly in lives and resources, but without producing victory. He said that such a war would be bitterly unpopular in this country, causing a political revolt. When asked how he could foresee such things, he replied:

> It wasn't a miracle — my anticipation of what would happen if we sent our armed forces into Vietnam without a declaration of war.
>
> When I opposed sending troops into Vietnam, I was not alone in my opposition. Both Senator Bob Taft, Sr., and General Douglas MacArthur were opposed to sending American troops into the jun-

gles of South Vietnam, where they would be bogged down and trapped in the jungles against the North Vietnamese, supplied with the most modern weapons by the Soviets and the Red Chinese.

I believed then that we couldn't win a war there.)

Hamilton Fish fears most fervently the acquisition, by whatever means — by fraud, by propaganda, by the manipulation of the media, the government, or the people themselves — of presidential power so strong as to set itself above Congress, the Constitution, or the will of the citizenry. That is why he continues to write and to speak out; for he believes, equally fervently, in the patriotism of Americans. He believes, and it is a faith neither cynical nor naive, but one based on realistic assessment, in the good will, the courage, and the native common sense inherent in all Americans. It is to these qualities that he appeals from the pinnacle (at which he would himself scoff) of his years and his experience.

The appeal is to be mindful and ever vigilant, to exercise the rights of a free people never to allow ourselves to be led astray against our wills, never to sacrifice for causes not our own, never to die in vain.

Hamilton Fish is a man who has lived for 94 years by the very words he used so eloquently in the Preamble to the American Legion Constitution: God, country, peace, freedom. This is what his long life has stood for. He asks only that we abide also.

The Publishers
February 1983

The young Hamilton Fish at eight years old: 1895.

Hamilton Fish, All-American tackle from Harvard: 1910. Also shown: his contemporary football great, the legendary Jim Thorpe.

HAMILTON FISH JR., now a member of congress from New York, first achieved fame as a Harvard tackle with a charge "like the recoil of a steel spring." In 1910 he was chosen by Walter Camp for an all-time All-American team.

JIM THORPE made football history at Carlisle, the federal Indian school at Carlisle, Pa. In 1911 he kicked four field goals in a game against Harvard. In 1912 he scored 25 touchdowns, kicked 37 extra points and three field goals.

Hamilton Fish, Jr.
For President

Extension of remarks

of

Hon. Harold Knutson

of Minnesota
in the
House of Representatives
Thursday, August 8, 1935

Letter from

Hon. Royal C. Johnson
a former Representative from South Dakota

(Not printed at Government expense)

United States
Government Printing Office
Washington : 1935

22772—11922

With General Douglas MacArthur in 1962, two
years before the General's death on April 5, 1964.

With President Dwight Eisenhower, Hon. Clare Boothe Luce, General Mark Clark, and former Ambassador to Switzerland Henry J. Taylor at the Order of Lafayette Freedom Award dinner: November 19, 1964.

Past National Commander of the American Legion. Fish was chairman of the Committee of Three that wrote the preamble to the Constitution of the American Legion in 1919.

The Honorable Hamilton Fish: historian, author, statesman, American freedom fighter.

TRAGIC
DECEPTION

INTRODUCTION

Over 40 years ago, President Franklin Roosevelt, using the vast power of his office, finally succeeded in involving the United States in war with Japan, to the furtherance of his ultimate goal: America's entrance into the European war. As Clare Luce said, he lied us into war with Germany through the back door.

From the very beginning of the war in Europe Roosevelt was determined that the United States should be a part of it. This in spite of the fact that 85 percent of the American people were opposed to sending American troops to fight in any foreign wars, let alone this major war, which in the end cost the United States 300,000 dead, 700,000 wounded, and half a trillion dollars.

The textbook reason for our entrance into World War II is the attack on Pearl Harbor by the Japanese. The facts, as they have come to light since then, prove otherwise.

President Roosevelt and Secretary of State Cordell Hull sent a deliberate war ultimatum to Japan ten days before Pearl Harbor. The message: Get your army, navy, air force, and police out of Vietnam and Manchuria (China). This left the Japanese the

3

choice of either committing suicide, surrendering, or fighting.

This "war" ultimatum was sent by Roosevelt the day after a secret meeting of his "war cabinet" at the White House on November 25, 1941. The war cabinet was an unofficial body, composed of interventionists. It functioned entirely separately from the actual Cabinet, though that group, too, contained two members who did not favor U.S. involvement in the European war: Charles Edison, former Democratic governor of New Jersey, and Henry Woodring, former Democratic governor of Kansas. They were eventually replaced by Henry L. Stimson and Frank Knox, both pro-war Republicans.

The war cabinet included, in addition to FDR, Secretary of State Hull, Secretary of War Stimson, Secretary of the Navy Knox, General George Marshall, and Admiral Harold Stark, all of them pro-war. The topic of their November 25th meeting was how to force, compel, goad, or trick Japan into war. The result was the ultimatum to Japan, not only to get out of Vietnam and China, but to break off relations with Germany. There is no question that the Japanese understood the intent of the demand. Two days later the President wondered aloud to Henry Stimson why the Japanese hadn't yet attacked us. He considered sending an even stronger ultimatum.

For many years, I, along with most Americans, believed the Roosevelt Administration's propaganda on the reasons we entered the war. As ranking Republican member of the Foreign Affairs and Rules Committees, I had led the fight in the House of

Representatives for several years to keep the President from involving us in the War. I had the support of 90 percent of the Republican House members, and probably half of the Democrats.

On December 8, the day after Pearl Harbor, I delivered the first speech ever made over radio from the House of Representatives. This speech, a declaration of war, upheld FDR's Day of Infamy proclamation, and denounced the Japanese as warmongers for attacking the United States while peace negotiations were still in progress. I pled for all non-interventionists in the United States to unite in supporting President Roosevelt and our armed forces for the defeat of the war-mad Japanese.

Once war had been declared, it would have been treasonous to expose the truth of how we became involved, even if anyone had known the facts at that time. As the truth gradually began to seep out, the Roosevelt administration set in motion the greatest propaganda machine ever devised in the United States. In essence, they produced a massive coverup of the facts, beginning with our issuance of a war ultimatum to Japan.

It is of historical importance to trace the events of December 6, the day before Pearl Harbor. Roosevelt had received from Japan the decoded answer to his war ultimatum. After reading it, he turned to Harry Hopkins and said: "This means war." The President, as Commander in Chief of the Armed Forces, should then have notified our officers in Hawaii and the Philippines, which he failed to do. Why? It can only be assumed that he did not *want* to stop an attack by the Japanese on the U.S. By then, the White House knew the Japanese fleet was moving toward Pearl Harbor. Had we been prepared to repel Japan's attack, FDR's excuse for getting us into the World War might have been lost. Not a single member of Congress had the slightest knowledge of the war ultimatum, Japan's response, or the subsequent coverup. To this day, many Americans still either do not know or refuse to face the truth.

In January 1982 ABC-TV produced an hour-long eulogy of Franklin Roosevelt to honor his centennial. The program was a spectacular glorification, produced from the viewpoint of FDR's New Deal cronies, of internationalists, and of pro-World War II advocates. I was amazed at the magnitude of this FDR propaganda, disseminated nationwide, which deliberately avoided telling the truth about our entrance into the War. The war ultimatum was, of course, never alluded to. The media apparently were only interested in lionizing Roosevelt. Exposure of the fact of the war ultimatum would not have served their purpose. A tribute to a President cannot very well point out that he lied and tricked the people into a major war.

FDR had been trying for over a year to get us into the European war, by attacking German submarines. Had he succeeded (in this effort) Hitler probably would not have attacked Stalin, who in turn might have remained neutral, perhaps even friendly to Germany. The three million German soldiers who were captured or killed in Russia, and the German artillery, airplanes, and tanks destroyed by the Soviets, would have been available to use against our armed forces, at a possible cost of several million Americans killed.

Why, after 40 years, do I feel it is so important that the truth of our participation in World War II become public knowledge? In an age when the nuclear destruction of the world could become reality in a moment, it is crucial to warn Americans against the kind of secret manipulation employed by Franklin Roosevelt to maneuver this country into war. Roosevelt's machinations have been studiously avoided by the press and television media. When I pointed out to the ABC television people, at their request, how Roosevelt had got us into war, not a single referral to what I said appeared in the FDR memorial broadcast. If left to the media, the truth might never be known.

Some may question my statements as an unjustified attack on a man many consider one of the greatest U.S. presidents. My answer is best expressed by quoting Theodore Roosevelt: "To announce that there must be no criticism of the President, right or wrong, is not only unpatriotic and servile, but it is morally treasonable to the American people. Nothing but the truth should be spoken about him or anyone else. But it is even more important to tell the truth, pleasant or unpleasant, about him than anyone else."

Why was Roosevelt, as President, pro-war? As Assistant Secretary of the Navy under Woodrow Wilson, he was greatly influenced by Wilson's pro-League of Nations and internationalist policies. In Wilson's second term, though he had promised to keep the U.S. out of war, we were fighting in Europe six months later. Wilson became the greatest advocate in both the United States and Europe for the League of Nations. FDR, as one of his appointees, accepted the internationalist ideology of his mentor.

By 1937, in his fourth year as President, Roosevelt was a committed internationalist. In his famous 1937 speech in Chicago, he proclaimed his faith in sanctions, embargoes, and various forms of policing the world. With this speech he assumed the leadership of internationalists and interventionists in the United States, Britain, and France. He formed a friendship with Winston Churchill, who had also become an international interventionist through his stance on defending the British Empire against an increasingly stronger and more powerful Germany under Hitler.

During 1938 and '39, while Joseph Kennedy was Ambassador to the Court of Saint James, the President threatened Prime Minister Neville Chamberlain to the effect that if he did not take a stronger stand against Germany, the United States would withdraw support from England. In fact, it was this threat that forced Chamberlain to take the fruitless position of assuring Poland of England's support in the event of war with Germany. This was a disastrous mistake. England could little afford to defend Poland, and she knew it.

However, Chamberlain's assurance did encourage the Polish Foreign Minister, Josef Beck, and the Polish generals, relying on the promise of English and French aid, to refuse a peaceful settlement of the Danzig issue, which became an important factor leading to the outbreak of the War. Although the Poles disliked Hitler and the Nazis, they hated Stalin and the communists more. Danzig's population was 90 percent German, and it voted overwhelmingly to return to Germany.

The voluminous number of messages between Roosevelt and Churchill, and statements made by Churchill, de Gaulle, and others in 1939, just after the German invasion, make very clear that both Churchill and de Gaulle believed that in case of war with Germany, Great Britain and France would have the open support of the United States.

Shortly before the outbreak of the War, I was elected president of the Congressional Interparliamentary Union, a group of twenty-four Congressmen and four Senators. We attended the meeting of the Interparliamentary Conference in Oslo two weeks before the war broke out. During this trip I stopped over in Paris where I met with (American) Ambassador Bullitt, French Foreign Minister Georges Bonnet, and the French Air Minister.

The head of the French Air Force was a comparatively young man, sure that war would break out with Germany within weeks. He believed firmly that the French Air Force was fully prepared for war. I tried to tell him that war would be a disaster for all the nations involved, that there would be enormous casualties and frightful destruction in lives and property. My arguments were wasted. This young Secretary had in the last few years revitalized the French Air Force, building and equipping numerous new aircraft. France assumed that it had an unbeatable air force. However, the tragedy was that neither the French, the British, nor the Americans believed Charles Lindbergh's report of the Germans' enormous and highly effective fleet of fighting aircraft. When the war broke out, the superior German air force smashed the French airplanes, opening the way for German tanks and armed forces to total victory. Lindbergh was telling the truth to promote the cause of peace. Instead, he was criticized as a Nazi sympathizer.

(Many distinguished members of Congress and other Americans who stood fearlessly against Roosevelt's efforts to get us into war were falsely maligned by the international and the eastern presses. These are the same newspapers who are today highly critical of members of Congress, the American Legion, and Veterans of Foreign Wars who, in the cause of peace, are urging the strenghtening of our defenses to prevent a nuclear holocaust.)

On the night of June 22, 1939, speaking as the ranking Republican on the House Foreign Affairs Committee, I delivered a nationwide NBC radio broadcast in which I said, "France lies prostrate and bleeding from the velvet glove and secret diplomacy pledges of President Roosevelt, which left her defenseless to her enemy because she has relied on his implied and false promises of support."

History now shows that Roosevelt, through Ambassador Bullitt in Paris, was largely responsible for plotting, prodding, and pushing France into war before she was adequately prepared, by secret promises of armed support from the U.S. I predicted many years ago that some day a disillusioned French statesman would tell the truth about the diplomatic duplicity and implied intervention. Georges Bonnet, French Foreign Minister in 1939 and for a number of years afterward, let the cat out of the diplomatic bag.

I received a letter from Bonnet from Paris, dated March 26, 1971. I knew him personally and had written asking if he would briefly state his views regarding the efforts made by Bullitt to influence the French government to assume a war stance against Hitler just prior to the beginning of the war. He replied:

> This is what I can tell you on this subject. As much as Bullitt counseled Daladier, the French premier, and myself [to have] prudence about the Czechoslovakia affair in 1938, he however in 1939 urged France to take a strong stand against Hitler. I am convinced also that he gave Daladier the conviction that Roosevelt would intervene [in the war] if he saw that France and England were in danger. I add that Bullitt held in large measure the illusion of many other people at that time, that Hitler was bluffing and that his army and aviation did not have the strength he pretended, and that he thought it would be enough to speak firmly to make him concede. I have no doubt whatsoever that this was his belief. . . . I will be, however, at your disposition to discuss these matters. One thing is certain is that Bullitt in 1939 did everything he could to make France enter the war.

Bonnet's statement only confirms my views on Bullitt's responsibility in urging France to go to war against Hitler. Ambassador Kennedy and Colonel Lindbergh both believed that Germany was far stronger than France both in air power and armaments. Unfortunately, FDR listened to Bullitt and downgraded the views of Kennedy and Lindbergh.

The morning following Roosevelt's press conference of April 13, 1940, the *New York Times* carried a front page story which began: "ROOSEVELT SEES AMERICA INVOLVED — President Roosevelt strongly implied that he believed that the involvement of the United States in any European war was inevitable and that this nation should stand shoulder to shoulder with Great Britain and France against Nazi-Fascist machinations."

There seems to be no question that FDR fully intended that the U.S. join England and France if they should go to war with Germany. The warhawks in these countries were given a salutary shot in the arm by FDR's implied war commitment. There could be only one interpretation in the minds of British and French officials — that the United States would join them promptly against any Nazi-Fascist aggression.

I

HOW THE UNITED STATES BECAME INVOLVED IN WORLD WAR II

President Roosevelt's responsibility for goading the Japanese into war by sending a war ultimatum on November 26, 1941, demanding that the Japanese withdraw all troops from Indo-China, and China (Manchuria) is an historical fact. The British cabinet was all for the appeasement of the Japanese prior to Hitler's invasion of Russia on June 22, 1941. After that it changed policy in a twinkling of an eye, as Churchill obtained FDR's promise that he would protect British interests in the Far East. Credit Churchill, Stalin, Owen Lattimore, Stimson, and Lauchlin Currie with assists in getting the United States into World War II through the back door.

Pitiless scrutiny and exposure should be turned on the actions of those responsible for serving a secret war ultimatum on Japan.

Admiral Kimmel and General Short should have been exonerated of any charges of dereliction of duty or errors of judgment. They were, as Admiral Halsey truthfully said, made the "scapegoats and were the martyrs" to protect the higher-ups who were responsi-

13

ble for the death of 3,000 American sailors and members of our armed forces at the terrible tragedy at Pearl Harbor. Years later Admiral Kimmel did not mince words when he said, "FDR and the top brass deliberately betrayed the American forces at Pearl Harbor,"[1] and that "FDR was the architect of the whole business. He gave presumably the orders that no word about the Japanese fleet movement was to be sent to Pearl Harbor, except by Marshall, and then he told Marshall not to send anything."[2]

Arthur Krock of the *New York Times* said to the President of the United States: "From the time of the quarantine speech in 1937 you have done everything possible to antagonize Japan and force it into the Axis . . ."

The alliance of Japan with the Axis powers was a bombshell to their opponents. Senator Nye declared, "Our foreign policy has succeeded in driving Japan into the arms of those who were the last ones we wanted her to associate with. Japan claimed it was due to the blunders of the United States State Department."

The Japanese would have done almost anything to avoid war with America. To protect their needed rice, rubber, and tin supplies, they got permission from Pétain's Vichy government to take over control of Vietnam. Naturally if Holland had refused to supply them with oil, they would have gone into the East Indies to be assured of a supply which was vital to their existence. They had no design on the Philippines or on any of our possessions. But as a nation they could not exist without oil for their industries, merchant marine,

[1]*Newsweek*, Dec. 12, 1966.
[2]The *New York Times*, Dec. 7, 1966.

and navy. Prince Kenoye, the prime minister, who was very peacefully inclined, repeatedly asked to come to Washington or Honolulu to meet with President Roosevelt. He was willing to agree to our terms to keep out of war on a *modus vivendi* but FDR refused to talk with the Japanese prime minister simply because he was determined to get into war with Japan, and, as a result, with Germany. The American ambassador in Tokyo, Joseph Grew, knew how much Japan wanted to maintain peaceful relations and urged such a conference. But FDR and his fellow interventionists used ruses, dodges, and tricks to involve us in a totally unnecessary war. Arthur Krock of the *New York Times* blamed FDR's drastic embargo policies for creating a war crisis and for forcing Japan to fight the United States.

It is utterly preposterous to say that Britain could hold Hong Kong, Singapore, Malaya, North Borneo and her other possessions in the Far East, yet deprive Japan of the right to purchase needed rice, oil, rubber, and other commodities. The Japanese would have signed any treaty and stopped any aggression to the south if they had been assured peacefully of buying rice and oil without which they could not exist as a first class nation.

It is true Japan had been engaged in an undeclared war with China for four years, but it was also true that Soviet Russia had been the aggressor against Finland, Poland and the Baltic nations. We not only did nothing about that, but later allied ourselves with the USSR. But Japan was willing to negotiate a withdrawal of its forces from China (not Manchuria) and also from Vietnam and agree not to move southward. What more could the United States ask from a powerful nation like Japan? Emperor Hirohito and Prime Minister Kenoye were willing to make incredible concessions to maintain peace.

Japan was a comparatively small nation of 80 million people, not quite as large as California, with very few natural resources and facing the constant threat of Soviet Russia, a ruthless neighbor. The emperor was a man of honor and peace who did his utmost to restrain the aggressive militarists around him.

The tragic war with Japan was unnecessary. It was a catastrophe for two nations that had much more to fear from communism than from each other. We not only gained nothing from the war, but lost a friendly China to the communists.

Britain lost much more, as she had special interests and privileges in China and lost Malaya, Singapore, Burma, India, and Ceylon.

Chiang Kai-shek was badly advised by Owen Lattimore in opposing the *modus vivendi* that called for the withdrawal of Japanese forces from China. That would have left Chiang Kai-shek in control of all of China. This was three years before the concessions made by Roosevelt to Stalin at Yalta. There would have been no reason for Stalin's Communist army, as our ally, to invade Manchuria. Chiang Kai-shek, as the friend of the United States, would have had all the arms and resources he needed to crush the Chinese Communist opposition.

The question is often raised, what would have happened if we had not entered the war, that is, if there had been no Japanese bombing of Pearl Harbor? The question deserves a detailed answer. I am convinced that we could easily have made a peace treaty with Japan in which she would have agreed to a mutually friendly withdrawal from China and Indochina in return for the right to trade with all nations in the Far East, including the Philippines and Dutch East Indies.

The extensive memoirs of Secretary of State Cordell Hull are a treasure-house of historical information, although naturally highly slanted in covering up his responsibility and that of FDR for the war ultimatum. In referring to the war ultimatum it seems appropriate to have it preceded by the word "infamous," derived from Roosevelt's designation of the attack on Pearl Harbor as a date to live in infamy.

Hull's memoirs do not even mention the crucial November 25 meeting at the White House. According to Stimson's diary, the only question considered at this meeting was how to maneuver, incite, and provoke Japan to fire the first shot. The next day Secretary Hull scrapped the *modus vivendi*, or ninety-day truce (which had been acceptable to Japan), and handed Ambassador Nomuro the infamous war ultimatum. It was not released until after Pearl Harbor, when it went unnoticed.

Admiral Nomuro was accompanied by Saburo Kurusu, who had served as a consul in New York and had recently been the Japanese ambassador to Berlin. He was married to an American, which gave him an added interest in maintaining friendly relations between Japan and the United States. After he had read Hull's proposals, Kurusu asked if this were the American

answer to the Japanese request for a *modus vivendi* or
truce. Secretary Hull gave an evasive and virtually
negative answer. Kurusu replied that the secretary's
statement was "tantamount to meaning the end." It
was obvious to Nomuro and Kurusu that this was a
war ultimatum and that the next step would be war.

The undisputed fact is that even those Japanese militarists who had no love for the United States realized
the tremendous potential strength of our country and
wanted to avoid such a ruinous war if a peace with
honor could be found. They were willing to make
unprecedented concessions and to accept virtually all
our terms in the proposed *modus vivendi*, which included
a ninety-day truce. For eight months Secretary Hull
had been stringing Ambassador Nomuro along, stalling
for time to permit our army and navy to strengthen
their defenses in the Philippines and in our other Far
Eastern possessions. Hull in his memoirs made it very
clear that he was playing for time at the request of both
the army and the navy. His dilatory tactics finally
became apparent to the Japanese cabinet, which set
November 29 as the final day for ending negotiations.
Hull knew definitely that the showdown on peace or
war had been reached through the intercepted Japanese
messages to Nomuro, as we had broken the Japanese
code.

Hull had been working on a *modus vivendi* which would
not only have postponed the war, but might have
averted an unwanted, unnecessary, costly and bloody
war with Japan completely. President Roosevelt
received protests from Churchill and Chiang Kai-shek.
FDR's administrative secretary, Lauchlin Currie, friendly to the communists, received an urgent cable from

Owen Lattimore, another apologist for communism. Lattimore had been appointed by Roosevelt as an adviser to Chiang Kai-shek. Naturally Soviet Russia was opposed to any peace terms and favored war between the United States and Japan.

Churchill realized, as did Roosevelt, that if we became involved in war with Japan it would automatically bring us into war with Germany. Consequently, the *modus vivendi* was scrapped.

Roosevelt used his tremendous presidential powers to deceive the American public. It was a conspiracy of silence. Later the administration refused to institute a nonpartisan, impartial court-martial of Admiral Kimmel and General Short, *at their own request,* to ascertain the true responsibility for the Pearl Harbor disaster. It was denied by the Roosevelt administration because it would have exposed FDR's ultimatum and likewise his responsibility for secretly provoking war.

Although the Congress was totally ignored, and only a handful of Americans in the cabinet knew of the existence of the war ultimatum, Winston Churchill and the British high command were kept informed of every move.

There were some ardent Anglophiles who believed it was America's function on any and all occasions to pull the chestnuts out of the fire for the British Empire. Just why Great Britain should have the unquestioned right to maintain numerous possessions in the Far East while Japan should be restricted by us, unable to even buy rice, oil, rubber, tin, and other commodities in nearby nations, is still an unsolved paradox.

The Japanese are a very sensitive, proud, courageous race imbued with a high sense of loyalty, honor and patriotism. Thirty-five years earlier, the Japanese navy had destroyed the Russian fleet, and its army had driven the Russians out of Manchuria. At the time of our drastic war ultimatum, the Japanese, after four years of war, controlled the seacoast, most of the large cities and a large part of China, and all of Manchuria to become the most powerful nation in the Far East.

Today, Japan is our best and most reliable friend in the Orient, whereas Soviet Russia, our former ally, has become our foe and an enemy of freedom throughout the world. The destinies of the United States and Japan are now linked together not only by bonds of friendship but by principles of freedom and democracy. The Japanese fought bravely to the end. Let us hope that there will never be another war between us, but that we will march forward, as two great nations, to preserve the freedom, the independence, and the sovereignty of both of our countries for eons of time. The entire world should know that we will keep our agreement for the defense of Japan if it is attacked. I was heartened when the *New York Post* on April 14, 1971, ran a picture of Norman Mineta, who as a child spent two years in a Japanese war relocation camp in the United States, accepting congratulations with his Japanese wife after winning an easy victory in the San Jose California mayoral race. He is the first Japanese-American to be elected mayor of a major American city.

*   *   *

The Roosevelt-Hull war ultimatum reached the emperor's palace on the morning of November 27 while a liasion conference was in session. It called for Japan to immediately "withdraw all military, naval, air, and police forces from China and Indochina, to support no other government or regime in China except Chiang Kai-shek," and, in effect, to abrogate the tripartite pact.

The Japanese construed China to include Manchuria, which they had no intention of giving up. If Hull had not meant "Manchuria" under the term "China," he should have made it clear at the time, not in an alibi afterwards. But Hull told Secretary of War Stimson the next day, "It is now in the hands of the army and navy."

It required no profound knowledge of Japanese history, institutions, and psychology to warrant three conclusions respecting the ultimatum. First, that no Japanese cabinet, liberal or reactionary, could have accepted its provisions as a basis of negotiating a settlement without incurring the risk of immediate overthrow. Second, that our State Department knew that the drastic ultimatum could not be accepted by the Japanese government as a program for renewed conversations "looking towards the maintenance of peace in the Pacific." And third, both President Roosevelt and Hull knew that the delivery of the war ultimatum to Japan would cause open warfare to begin without any declaration of war.

II

THE TRAGEDY OF PEARL HARBOR

All Americans, including myself, joined President Roosevelt in denouncing the attack on Pearl Harbor by the Japanese as a Day of Infamy. Every American was shocked by such a dastardly, unprovoked attack.

As ranking Republican member of the Committee on Rules, I opened the debate on Monday, December 8th, 1941, for the declaration of war resolution against Japan. My speech was not only the first one, but it was also the first speech ever delivered over the radio in the House of Representatives.

I am ashamed of that speech today as I now know about Roosevelt's infamous war ultimatum that forced Japan's leaders to fight. At that time I did not mince words and was proud of my remarks. Here is my speech as then delivered.

DECLARATION OF WAR
An Appeal for National Unity in America
and for War to Final Victory
Declaration of War Speech
of
Hon. Hamilton Fish
of New York
In the House of Representatives
Monday, December 8, 1941

MR. FISH. Mr. Speaker, it is with sorrow and deep resentment against Japan that I rise to support a declaration of war.

I have consistently opposed our entrance into wars in Europe and Asia for the past 3 years but the unwarranted, vicious, brazen and dastardly attack by the Japanese Navy and Air Force while peace negotiations were pending at Washington and in defiance of the President's eleventh-hour personal appeal to the Emperor, makes war inevitable and necessary.

The time for debate and controversy within America has passed. The time for action has come.

Interventionists and noninterventionists must cease criminations and recriminations, charges and countercharges against each other, and present a united front behind the President and the Government in the conduct of the war.

There can be only one answer to the treacherous attack of the Japanese, and that is war to final victory, cost what it may in blood and treasure and tears. This unprovoked and senseless aggression by the Japanese armed forces upon our possessions must be answered by war.

Although I have consistently fought against our intervention in foreign wars, I have repeatedly stated that if we were attacked by any foreign nation, or if the Congress of the United States declared war in the American and constitutional way, I would support the President and the administration to the bitter end.

Whom the gods would destroy they first make mad. The Japanese have gone stark raving mad and have by their unprovoked attack committed military, naval and national suicide.

I shall at the proper time volunteer my services as an officer in a combat division, as I did in the last war, preferably with colored troops.

There is no sacrifice too great that I will not make in defense of America and to help annihilate these war-mad Japanese devils.

Now that we are to fight let us go in with our heads and chins up in the American way, and let us serve notice upon the world that this is not only a war against aggression and in defense of our own territories, but a war for freedom and democracy all over the world, and that we will not stop until victory is won.

I appeal to all American citizens, particularly to the members of my own party, and to noninterventionists, to put aside personal views and partisanship, and unite behind the President, our Commander in Chief, in assuring victory to the armed forces of the United States.

Our country! In her intercourse with foreign nations, may she always be right, but right or wrong, our country!

Roosevelt's Day of Infamy statement has been turned into hypocrisy, deceit, and ashes by the searchlight of truth on the causes , events, and results of the war.

The tragic part of this unnecessary war was that the Japanese government and people, as reported consistently by our Ambasador Joseph Grew, a career diplomat of high integrity and intelligence, did not want war. The American people certainly did not want war with Japan. The rabid internationalists, however, believed that it was our manifest duty and mission to police the world, almost single-handed, no matter what the cost in lives and treasure, and against the will of an overwhelming majority of the American people and the Congress of the United States.

Many books and thousands of pages by investigating committees are available to all historians and students about the Pearl Harbor tragedy. One thing is certain —that the Roberts Commission appointed by the president immediately afterwards was a committee specially selected by those who had been instrumental in sending the war-provoking ultimatum to Japan on November 26, 1941, ten days before the attack. Most of the testimony taken by this commission has been repudiated by the army, navy and congressional committees and tends to show that Roosevelt, Stimson, and Knox who were responsible for the appointees, sought *to cover up their part in tricking the American people into war.* The separate army and navy investigations and reports exonerated Admiral Kimmel and General Short of dereliction of duty and placed the blame squarely on Secretary Hull, General Marshall, and Admiral Stark for not notifying Admiral Kimmel and General Short of the imminence of war on the morning of December 6.

These army and navy reports were held up by War Secretary Stimson and Navy Secretary Knox for some time, until public opinion finally forced their publication. Both the army and navy boards should be commended for the courage they demonstrated in their investigations, which placed the blame on the higher-ups in Washington. Secretaries Stimson and Knox only escaped condemnation because of their respective positions as Secretaries of War and Navy, as did President Roosevelt, their Commander in Chief.

By the time the reports were issued FDR and Knox were dead, but Hull, Stimson, Marshall and Stark were alive. Stimson was more to blame than anyone, except the President and Hull, for the drastic war ultimatum. He even advised Roosevelt that if the Japanese did not attack, *we* should do so immediately.

Naturally when the army report condemning Hull and Marshall was publicized throughout the country, Stimson rushed to their defense (actually to his own defense as he was equally to blame). Why? Because it was absolutely necessary to hide from the public their part in the secret war-provoking ultimatum.

Why did General Marshall and Admiral Stark delay in sending messages to the American Hawaiian commanders immediately after the ultimatum was issued, especially as soon as they knew of the intercepted Japanese repudiation of the ultimatum either the evening of the December 6 or the morning of December 7? Did Roosevelt contact General Marshall on the evening of December 6? And if not, why not? Admiral Stark was at the theater when the information reached the president. Both Marshall and Stark were pro-war and joined Secretary Stimson and Secretary Knox in a strange silence, still unaccounted for. Why did they not notify Kimmel and Short of the repudiation of the ultimatum indicating that Pearl Harbor might be attacked by Japan immediately?

The delay and virtual refusal to inform our Hawaiian commanders is inconceivable, except as a part of a deceitful and concerted scheme of silence.

I have read numerous books and reports of hearings before Congress, and they have always ignored the implications of the war ultimatum. After all, FDR was the recognized head of the Democratic party and his responsibility for issuing the ultimatum would have been equivalent to holding him responsible for the disaster at Pearl Harbor (which of course he was).

The tragedy of Pearl Harbor rests with FDR, not only because of the infamous war ultimatum, but for not making sure that Kimmel and Short were notified of the Japanese answer to the ultimatum. Subsequently Short and Kimmel were smeared and dismissed, presumably in order to clear President Roosevelt and his war cabinet of their responsibility.

Rear Admiral Robert A. Theobald (U.S.N. Ret.) published a very carefully documented book, *The Final Secret of Pearl Harbor*. In this book he confirmed that Roosevelt started the war. He also claimed that FDR assisted in the secret plans of leaving Pearl Harbor open for a surprise attack by not telling Admiral Stark and General Marshall to warn Admiral Kimmel and General Short of the contents of the decoded Japanese messages about the location of American warships in Pearl Harbor and Japan's final answer to his war-provoking ultimatum.

Secretaries Stimson and Knox, both so anxious for war, did nothing. Their official spokesmen, General Marshall and Admiral Stark, likewise remained silent regarding the ultimatum. All of them, from the President down, refrained from sending direct warnings, or seeing that they were sent to Admiral Kimmel and General Short. Secretary Hull apparently did nothing either, and he must have known of the intercepted messages of December 6. He was probably the first to receive such messages, and may have been the one who sent FDR the intercepted reply to the ultimatum.

Although Hull is to blame, next to FDR, he had no

direct responsibility for notifying the Hawaiian commanders. However, he should have informed Stimson and Knox immediately, and he may very well have done so. But Hull was also one of the collaborators bound to silence and was as much involved as anyone.

Admiral Theobald asserted definitely that Marshall was not out riding on the morning of December 7, but was in Admiral Stark's office discussing the decoded Japanese answer to the ultimatum. When Stark offered to notify Admiral Kimmel, Marshall said that he would do it, which he proceeded to do later on, with a belated message, received long after the attack. Under the circumstances, General Marshall's stupidity or his deliberate silence is incomprehensible unless he was acting on orders from President Roosevelt, as Admiral Theobald claims he was.

Admiral Kimmel and General Short, according to Admiral Halsey, were scapegoats, sacrificed on the political scaffold in order to protect the guilty parties. The President appointed the Roberts Commission to investigate Kimmel and Short, but not his own infamous secret ultimatum.

President Roosevelt made sure that the records would not disclose his war ultimatum, by appointing Supreme Court Justice Owen Roberts, a Republican. He was just as outspoken a pro-war zealot as Stimson and Knox, and an advocate of "Union Now." He was recommended by Stimson to serve as chairman of the commission. Knox and Stimson recommended the army and navy personnel of that commission. Naturally the tragic war ultimatum was hushed up, and the entire responsibility for the disaster at Pearl Harbor was placed on Admiral Kimmel and General Short.

Admiral Halsey, one of our greatest fighting admirals and one of the three senior commanders of the Pacific Fleet serving under Admiral Kimmel at Pearl Harbor, had this to say in a foreword to *The Final Secret of Pearl Harbor:*

> Had we known of Japan's minute and continued interest in the exact location and movement of our ships at Pearl Harbor as indicated in the "magic messages" (which were never sent to Admiral Kimmel) it is only logical that we would have concentrated our thought on meeting the practical certainty of an attack on Pearl Harbor . . . If the magic messages had been known to us, there can be no doubt that a 360-degree search would have been ordered and maintained to the breaking point of material and personnel.
>
> I have always considered Admiral Kimmel and General Short to be splendid officers *who were thrown to the wolves as scapegoats* for something over which they had no control. They had to work with what they were given, both in equipment and information. *They are our outstanding militay martyrs.* —William F. Halsey, Fleet Admiral, U.S. Navy, Fishers Island, September 1953.

This testimony of one of our greatest war heroes makes it very clear that Admiral Kimmel and General Short were not alerted after the war ultimatum was sent to Japan, and even more important, they were not told that Japan had repudiated the ultimatum.

Admiral Kimmel, referring to *The Final Secret of Pearl Harbor,* said his studies have caused him to conclude "that we were unready at Pearl Harbor because of *President Roosevelt's plans that no word be sent to alert the fleet at Hawaii . . ."*

Kimmel was emphatic that the "individuals in high positions in Washington who willfully refrained from alerting our forces at Pearl Harbor, should never be excused." Later he denounced FDR as being responsible.

President Roosevelt evidently did not want to take any steps that might prevent an attack by the Japanese, because if the Japanese knew in advance that we had been warned and were prepared, the attack on Pearl Harbor would have been called off.

Kimmel and Short, as longtime distinguished officers in our armed forces, were entitled to a court-martial. This was consistently denied them. The administration knew that in an impartial court-martial both officers would subpoena witnesses and cross-examine them and that the whole truth about the war ultimatum would be brought out.

On June 5, 1944, speaking in the House of Representatives, I said that there had already been too much delay and shadowboxing by the Roosevelt administration to avoid telling the whole truth to the American people and, more important, in holding those responsible for the Pearl Harbor disaster strictly accountable:

> Mr. Speaker, I propose to read an editorial taken from the *World Telegram,* a Scripps-Howard paper in New York. If I should use the same words someone might accuse me of making a political speech or injecting politics into our war efforts. This paper is one of the

largest in the city of New York, and the same editorial was probably circulated widely over the country. It is entitled "Kimmel, Short, Roosevelt, Hull." Mr. Speaker, the administration should have held the Pearl Harbor court-martial long ago. The editorial stated, "The administration is plainly resolved to postpone the Pearl Harbor trials until after the election. The Japs have long known exactly what they did to us in that most disgraceful disaster ever suffered by American arms. To hold the trials now would tell them nothing they didn't know already.

"But it is widely believed that the trials would force to light evidence connecting high Washington officials with orders to Kimmel and Short to take the No. 1 alert (readiness to sabotage from within) instead of No. 3 (readiness for anything) which might have turned Pearl Harbor into a victory for us and shortened the Pacific war. These orders might have been urged by Mr. Hull, or send by Mr. Roosevelt.

"If such orders were sent (alert No. 1), the administration is determined to keep the American people from knowing who sent them until after the election. Politics and politics alone is the cause of this procrastination."

Mr. Speaker, those are not my words. They are from an editorial in one of our largest newspapers, a more or less nonpartisan paper that reflects, I believe, public sentiment throughout the United States.

The Roberts report was so slanted and outrageous that public opinion demanded further investigation. A congressional committee was created consisting of Senators Barkley, George and Lucas (Democrats), and Senators Brewster and Ferguson (Republicans), Representatives Cooper, Clarke, and Murphy (Democrats) and Gerhart and Keefe (Republicans).

Two of the three Democratic members of the committee, Senators Barkley of Kentucky and Lucas of Illinois, were both candidates for the vice-presidency. FDR was not only the leader of the Democratic Party, but controlled the Democratic national organization that nominated the presidential candidates.

The following well-known ditty fits the political situation confronted by the Democratic members of the congressional investigating committee:

> Mother, may I go in to swim?
> Yes, my darling daughter.
> Hang your clothes on a hickory limb.
> But don't go near the water.

The "water" here was FDR's secret war ultimatum. The composition of the Democratic majority was part of the coverup of Roosevelt, come hell or high water. Naturally Senator Robert Reynolds, chairman of the Military Affairs Committee or Senator David Walsh, chairman of the Navel Affairs Committee, were not on the committee; they were both outspoken noninterventionists and would have conducted an impartial investigation that let the chips fall where they may.

Three out of the four Democratic investigating committee members came from the South and were ardent Roosevelt followers in both war and peace. The fourth, from the North, was a politically ambitious candidate for president or vice-president who naturally followed the Roosevelt line. However, the Congressional Joint Investigating Committee was fair in repudiating the actions of the Roberts Commission in finding Kimmel and Short guilty of dereliction of duty. This was changed into failure of the commanders in errors of judgment. To this extent, they lifted the stigma of dereliction placed on the officers by Roosevelt's Roberts Commission. Two Republican members of the House, one of whom wrote a separate report, were defeated for reelection in their congressional districts. The pro-war interventionist Democrats on the Committee did everything·they could to protect Roosevelt and the members of his war cabinet. The real key to the Hawaiian disaster, the infamous war ultimatum, was swept under the rug.

Senator Brewster of Maine and Senator Ferguson of Michigan, members of the Congressional Investigating Committee, signed a minority report placing the blame for the Pearl Harbor tragedy squarely on Roosevelt, Hull, Stimson, Knox, Marshall, and Stark. But Admiral Kimmel's demand for a court-martial, supported by a congressional resolution, was sidetracked by the administration.

Speaking in Congress on June 5, 1944, I made specific predictions which have been verified and borne out by subsequent events:

MR. FISH: Mr. Speaker, Admiral Kimmel has demanded a free and open trial, and I am sure, knowing General Short as I do, having served on his staff in the 1940 maneuvers held in northern New York State, that he is the type of man who would like to have a free and open trial immediately. However, I do not believe that this court-martial will ever be held in spite of a congressional resolution or anything the Congress does or says, at least until after election, and then there is some uncertainty of its ever being held until a new administration takes over at Washington.

MR. SHORT: If it is not held it will not be the fault of Congress if we pass this resolution.

MR. FISH: That is true. I want to make another prediction. If the administration holds a trial and Admiral J. O. Richardson is called as a witness, the public will find out that he protested placing our warships in Pearl Harbor, where they could be picked off like a lot of sitting ducks, as they were on the seventh of December 1941. Admiral Richardson was in command of the Pacific Fleet and was removed from office because he resisted the orders from President Roosevelt to take his fleet into Pearl Harbor and was succeeded by Admiral Kimmel. I think the American people will be surprised and shocked if Admiral Richardson ever appears before a court-martial and testifies to the whole truth, which he will be required to do as a witness. That is the kind of information the American people want and are entitled to, but probably will never get.

FDR was evidently thinking of getting into war with Japan as far back as October 8, 1940, when he told Admiral Richardson, then in charge of the fleet at the Hawaiian base, that sooner or later the Japanese would make a mistake and we would enter the war. That was a year and two months before Pearl Harbor.

At the Atlantic Conference, August 1941, President Roosevelt conferred with Prime Minister Churchill regarding an agreement to protect the British interests in the Far East; the proceedings have never been released to the American public. Churchill's statement to Parliament on January 27, 1942, verified this agreement: "The probability since the Atlantic Conference at which I discussed these matters with President Roosevelt, that the United States *even if not herself attacked would come into the war in the Far East* and thus make victory sure, seemed to allay some of the anxieties." [Author's italics]

Secretary Stimson was so anxious to get into the war that he conjured up limitless war powers for the President in defiance of the Congress and the Constitution. He claimed that the president had power to inform a foreign government that if terms he determined were not accepted and obeyed that the president had power to order war on any government without any declaration of war by Congress. The legality of Stimson's views was distorted at best; such claims ignored the Congress and the Constitution completely.

The Congress under the Constitution provides for our national defense and has the sole power to declare war, but the Constitution does not state that a president can use any pretext he wants to secretly trick the American people into war.

The reports of both the army and navy boards are a living testimony of the high character, integrity and honor of our army and navy officers. All members of these boards knew they were jeopardizing their own

careers by telling the truth, and blaming those responsible in Washington, in direct opposition to their superior officers, the secretaries of war and navy.

What has impressed me in reading and studying the
testimony in most of the investigations and particularly
their recommendations, is that those naval officers
who were present at Hawaii and who knew the situation firsthand have been the most outspoken in support
of Admiral Kimmel and in blaming their superiors,
General Marshall and Admiral Stark, in Washington.

Admiral Halsey said in his foreword to Admiral
Theobald's book, *The Final Secret of Pearl Harbor,* that every
American who believes in fair play should read it. The
thesis of Admiral Theobald's book is that FDR alone
was responsible for the helplessness of the Pacific Fleet
and the unpreparedness at Hawaii, not Admiral Kimmel and General Short. Admiral Theobald was at Pearl
Harbor on the fatal day and like most naval officers, he
is of unimpeachable character and integrity. Admiral
Halsey also did not mince words when he stated in the
foreword, "We were sadly deficient in long-range
scouting planes. The only army planes available were
B-18's. These planes were slow, short legged, and unfit-
ted for overseas scouting."

*   *   *

FDR in an address to the nation said: "I tell you the
blunt fact that the German submarine fired first upon
the American destroyer without warning and with
deliberate design to sink her."

The Senate Committee on Naval Affairs headed by

Senator Walsh of Massachusetts crossexamined Admiral Stark and discovered that FDR's statement was completely erroneous. The American destroyer *Greer* had trailed the German submarine for three hours, reporting its position to a British plane which finally attacked with depth charges. The submarine had fired at the *Greer* only after the plane departed to refuel and the *Greer* had actively continued the hunt alone. It was at the time of the attack on the *Greer* that FDR issued the "shoot first" orders. The report of the Naval Affairs Committee was not issued until much later. The alleged attack on the SS *Kearny* was likewise deceptively presented to the American people.

The fact is that the *Kearny* had dropped depth bombs on a German submarine which later retaliated. These are merely examples of FDR's attempts to mislead and misrepresent the facts and thereby stir up an emotional flame of hatred against the Germans, all of which was a part of his consistent campaign of deception.

Two months before Pearl Harbor Roosevelt issued orders to shoot at German ships and submarines at sight. But Hitler ordered his navy to avoid attacking American vessels and only to defend themselves. This ruined FDR's plans to provoke Germany. Consequently Japan was made the scapegoat and war target. Admiral Stark, then chief of Naval Operations, in reply to a question before the Joint Congressional Committee investigating the naval disaster at Pearl Harbor said: "Technically, or from an international standpoint, we were not at war, inasmuch as we did not have the right of belligerents, because war had not been declared. But actually, so far as the forces operating under Admiral

King in certain areas (European zone), it was against any German craft that came inside that area."

A combination of Admiral Stark's testimony and the infamous ultimatum to Japan proves beyond any reasonable doubt that FDR sought to get us into war, and finally succeeded.

The intense pro-Roosevelt apologists may try to defend his un-American, undemocratic and unconstitutional methods of provoking war. They will probably say that the end justifies the means and he knew best what was in the interests of the nation. That doctrine is a total repudiation of our democratic institutions and representative and constitutional form of government. It violates Lincoln's "government of the people, by the people and for the people." It turned to ashes the principles and policies of neutrality and peace established by Washington, and upheld by Jefferson, Jackson, and Theodore Roosevelt. It makes a joke of the great constitutional speeches and legacies of Hamilton, Madison, Jay, Marshall, Clay, and Webster. FDR's clandestine foreign policy spurned the Congress and created a near dictatorship. It disavowed our Declaration of Independence, which repudiated the divine right of any one man to declare war.

I recommend for further reading, *The Final Secret of Pearl Harbor* by Rear Admiral Robert A. Theobald. (Old Greenwich, Conn.: Devin-Adair, Publishers, 1954) Some extracts from this book showing the American moves which led to the Japanese attack, are herewith included.

President Roosevelt's conversation with Admiral Richardson in October 1940 indicated his conviction that it would be impossible without a stunning incident to obtain a declaration of war from Congress.

Despite the conditions of undeclared war which existed in the Atlantic during the latter half of 1941, it had long been clear that Germany did not intend to contribute to the creation of a state of formal war between her and the United States. The stoppage of Philippine exports to Japan via executive order on May 29, 1941;

The freezing of Japanese assets and the interdiction of all trade with Japan by the United States, Great Britain, and the Netherlands, on July 25th, 1941.

The termination of the Washington Conference of Nov. 26, 1941, when Secretary Hull handed Admiral Nomuro the famous war provoking ultimatum, unknown to Congress or to the American people until after the attack on Pearl Harbor.

President Roosevelt and his military and naval advisers were well aware that Japan invariably started her wars with a surprise attack synchronized closely with her delivery of a declaration of war.

The retention of the fleet in Hawaii, especially after its reduction in strength in March 1941 could serve only one purpose, an invitation to a surprise Japanese attack.

The denial to the Hawaiian commanders of all knowledge of magic was vital to the plans of enticing Japan to deliver a surprise attack upon the fleet at Pearl Harbor.

Everyone familiar with Japanese military history knew that her first acts of war against China in 1894 and Russia in 1904 have been surprise attacks against the main fleets of those countries. The only American naval force in the Pacific that was worth the risk of such an operation was the fleet in Hawaiian waters.

A Tokyo dispatch to the Japanese Embassy at Washington on Nov. 28th definitely stated that the Japanese Government considered that the American note of the 26th had terminated all possibility of further negotiations.

The Japanese code destruction messages of December 1st and 2nd meant that war was extremely close at hand.

With the distribution of the pilot message at three P.M. on Saturday, Dec. 6, the picture was complete for President Roosevelt and other recipients of "magic."

Never before in reported history had a Field Commander been denied information that his country would be at war in a couple of hours and that everything pointed to a surprise attack upon his forces shortly after sunrise. No naval officer on his own initiative would ever make such a decision as Admiral Stark thus did.

That fact and Admiral Stark's decisions on that Sunday morning even if they had not been supported by the wealth of earlier evidence, would reveal beyond question the basic truth of the Pearl Harbor story, i.e., that these Sunday messages and so many earlier ones of vital importance to Admiral Kimmel's exercise of his command were not sent because Admiral Stark had orders from the President which prohibited that action.

This deduction is fully supported by the Admiral's statement to the press in August 1945 that all he did during the pre-Pearl Harbor days was done on order of higher authority, which can only mean, President Roosevelt. The most arresting thing he did during that time was to withhold information from Admiral Kimmel.

Speech of Hon. Dewey Short (Republican) of Missouri in the House of Representatives on November 28, 1944, three years after the attack on Pearl Harbor:

Mr. Speaker: Truth tho crushed to earth will rise again and like murder tho it hath no tongue will speak in a most miraculous way. The American people have not been told the truth about Pearl Harbor. They want to know the truth and are entitled to know it in the name of both the living and the dead. Some day we will know it, and though from my exasperating and painful experience with this particular matter, I dare not prophecize [sic] when, but I repeat, sir, some day we will know the complete story and the whole truth about the most painful and disgraceful defeat of our armed forces in the annals of our country.

And when the complete story is told and the whole truth known, the American people will be shocked, angered, and grieved — deeply grieved and sorely wounded. Perhaps we shall have to wait for future historians to place the responsibility for this most tragic chapter of our nation's history but that does not relieve us from at least attempting to do our duty now. We certainly should assert every effort to prevent a replica of the Dreyfus case in the United States with all its unfortunate implications.

III

HOW ROOSEVELT PRODDED
THE BRITISH GOVERNMENT
INTO WAR

The full extent of the American diplomatic intervention and international prodding of England, France, and Poland prior to the outbreak of World War II, is still little known, particularly the aggressive activities of our ambassador to Paris, William Bullitt, who was FDR's spokesman in Europe.

The following is an extract from an interesting article by Drew Pearson and Robert S. Allen, dated April 14, 1939, that might well be entitled, "How Roosevelt and the State Department Served an Ultimatum on Prime Minister Chamberlain."

The authors were interventionists and friendly to the Roosevelt administration. It is historically important to relate what they said at that time to show how far President Roosevelt went to influence British diplomacy in 1938 and 1939, to turn Britain from peaceful negotiation with Germany into war.

The State Department has just heaved big sighs of relief after terminating one of the most crucial episodes

42

of international prodding. The objective of the State Department, or perhaps it is more accurate to say of the president himself, has been to push, goad, or cajole the British Empire into the realization that democracy is at stake in Europe. [*Author's note:* What happened to the democracies and free nations of Europe — Poland, Czechoslovakia, Hungary, the Baltic and Balkan nations?] All this took place during the period of diplomatic double-crossing in which British banks actually were lending money to Germany for rearmament and the Federation of British Industries were negotiating a secret pact with German industries in violation of the Anglo-American agreement.

These double-crossings finally became so flagrant that when Roosevelt, Hull and Welles got the full drift of it, they sent a virtual ultimatum to Chamberlain declaring that as far as the U.S. was concerned, Great Britain was either a Nazi nation or a democracy, and that the United States would watch Chamberlain's future policy for the answer. To get the full picture of British double-crossing and to understand what led up to this crisis in Anglo-American relations, it is necessary to trace the events after the Munich crisis last October (1938).

After Munich, the Roosevelt administration instructed Ambassador Joe Kennedy to suggest to Chamberlain that the only thing Hitler understood was the straight arm and that it would be an excellent idea to call an abrupt halt on appeasement. Supposedly Chamberlain agreed, whereupon Roosevelt and his State Department mapped out a program carefully calculated to show Hitler that he could give the democracies no more lip. [*Author's note:* The Communists made mincemeat of the democracies of eastern and southeastern Europe.] To this end the United States deliberately recalled the ambassador from Berlin, [*Author's note:* A bad blunder as we were unable to exert any influence in Germany for peace just before the outbreak of World War II] and deliberately planned that Secretary Ickes should scold the German chargé d'affaires for his effrontery in protesting. It was no accident that Roosevelt's address to Congress on the State of the Union vigorously slapped down the dictators.

Later it was discovered that whenever the State Department would take a stern stand against Hitler, Sir John Simon or other Tory members of the British Cabinet would trot around to the Nazis and tell them that Britain was not in sympathy with the United States pronouncements. Finally, just before the last Czech crisis, the State Department learned that the powerful Federation of British Industries in which several cabinet members were represented, had worked out a secret trade agreement with the Nazis, undercutting the United States and the Anglo-American trade agreement so laboriously negotiated by Cordell Hull.

By this time the sentiment of Roosevelt, Hull, et al., towards the British would have burnt up the printed pages. Their almost inescapable conclusion was that the oligarchy, which actually rules Britain at heart, was anxious to preserve the dictators and secretly feared the strengthening of democratic governments similar to the popular front in France or the Negrin Regime in Spain.

The Pearson-Allen article was published four and a half months before the start of the European war, and inserted in the Congressional Record. It proves to what an extent President Roosevelt prodded, pushed, and goaded Prime Minister Chamberlain and his cabinet. It shows how far we interfered with and influenced the British foreign policy from negotiation with Germany into the most bloody, costly, and disastrous war in the history of the world — one that left half of Europe bled white, ruined, and devastated, and the democracies of eastern Europe overwhelmed by communist dictatorships.

England itself was a major victim, both in blood and treasure. She was virtually bankrupt after six years of war, and had lost a large part of her Empire.

The statement by two American columnists, both ardent supporters of the Roosevelt administration, clearly sets forth the brazen attempts of FDR for more than a year before the outbreak of World War II, not only to influence, but to dictate the policies of the British government regarding Germany.

If President Roosevelt could dictate to the prime minister of Britain, he could, and did, do the same to the prime ministers and foreign ministers of both France and Poland, through his main spokesman, William Bullitt, who although our ambassador to France, was also FDR's roving ambassador extraordinary for all of Europe.

IV
"YOUR BOYS ARE NOT GOING TO BE SENT INTO ANY FOREIGN WARS"

Noninterventionists who had naturally suspected President Roosevelt ever since his quarantine speech of October 7, 1937, were confirmed in their opposition to him by his selection of Henry Stimson as Secretary of War and Frank Knox as Secretary of the Navy. Both of them were leaders in the Republican war camp. Stimson was a warmaker par excellence. He made no attempt to conceal his views.

On June 18, 1940, Stimson delivered a radio speech that was virtually in favor of an undeclared war. He urged opening our ports to British and French war vessels and sending our own ships into the war zones as convoys. Exactly at this time, Stimson was invited to serve as Secretary of War. Before accepting, he asked President Roosevelt over the telephone whether he had read the text of his speech. The President replied that he had read the speech and approved of it. Of course the public did not know this, but they did know of Stimson's strong wish for war.

The insincerity and barefaced dishonesty of FDR's subsequent peace promises constituted an all-time high of misrepresentation, hypocrisy, and deception of the American people. At the end of the 1940 presidential campaign, the Democratic leaders, fearing the strong peace vote, urged Roosevelt to counteract it by making a powerful peace plea. This was the origin of the most shocking, contemptible, and untruthful public utterance of any president in our history.

It was in Boston on October 30, 1940, a week before the election that he said, "While I am talking to you mothers and fathers, I give you one more assurance. I have said this before, but I shall say it again and again and again: Your boys are not going to be sent into any foreign wars."

On November 3, a few days before his third-term election over Wendell Willkie, he added, "The first purpose of our foreign policy is to keep our country out of war."

These outright peace promises and pledges coming from the president of the United States were believed and acclaimed by voters in every village, hamlet, town, and city in the country. Wendell Willkie, the Republican candidate, was pursuing a zig-zag course between peace and war and ended up running the wrong way with the peace ball. He was nominated by the internationalist Republican warmakers and did not dare to denounce the Democratic war party or President Roosevelt. He conducted a shadow-boxing campaign regarding the peace issue, the issue closest to the hearts and minds of the great majority of the electorate.

Roosevelt's deliberate deception on a matter involving the life or death of hundreds of thousands of young Americans was unforgivable, unforgettable, and unconscionable. Before making such total peace promises, even *while* making them, he was using his vast powers to involve the United States in another European war. Certainly the American people should take another look at his Boston promise — "Your boys are not going to be sent into any foreign wars." He omitted the words, "except in case of attack," which were always used by antiwar and noninterventionist speakers.

Robert Sherwood, who suggested the all-out peace pledge for Roosevelt's Boston speech, wrote years later, "I burn inwardly whenever I think of those words, again — and again — and again."

President Roosevelt and those associated with him never sought to apologize to the American people. But by his secret ultimatum to Japan he did send ten million American soldiers, sailors, and marines to fight in foreign lands.

FDR's peace assurance outpromised, outpledged, and outdeceived any other public statement ever made by a president. Why did he make it? Because he was determined to get elected by hook or crook, so that he could carry out his obsession, to take the American people into World War II. Remember that he said just days before his election, "The first purpose of our foreign policy is to keep our country out of war." This is the same president who issued a drastic war ultimatum a year later to the Japanese government for the sole purpose of forcing Japan, like a cornered rat, to fight and fire the first shot.

Two months after his pre-election promise to the American fathers and mothers that their sons would not be sent into any foreign wars, FDR sent Harry

Hopkins, his alter ego, to London to tell Churchill a different story. "The President is determined that we shall win the war together. Make no mistake about it. He has sent me here to tell you that at all costs and by all means he will carry you through . . . There is nothing that he will not do, so far as he has human power."

Harry Hopkins pledged American support to Britain at an official dinner. He quoted from the Book of Ruth: "Wither thou goest, I will go, and where thou lodgest, I will lodge . . . . Where thou diest, I will die."

Robert E. Sherwood, Roosevelt's main ghost-writer, condoned Roosevelt's repeated deception of the American people by saying: "The inescapable fact is that this was what Roosevelt was compelled to say in order to maintain any influence over public opinion and over Congressional action." Deception is another word for coverup.

A number of distinguished and loyal Americans honestly believed that we should have entered the European war at the outset when Poland was invaded by Hitler, or at least when France was invaded and conquered. But most public opinion in the United States opposed our involvement in another world war even at those times.

I have no quarrel with any American who honestly believed it was in our interest to enter the war in Europe when Hitler's armies invaded Poland on September 1, 1939. That is the right of all Americans under the free speech guarantee in the Constitution, but it works both ways — for war interventionists and non-interventionists alike.

The question is sincerely raised: why didn't we enter

the war in the beginning when Poland was attacked? The answer is that most Americans did not know the cause of the war or even where Danzig was. The Congress, under the Constitution, has the sole power to declare war. At that time over 96 percent of the American people, and the Congress, were opposed to joining another European war. Seven months later when Hitler's armed forces invaded Norway, a Gallup poll showed 3 percent of the American people in favor of entering the war and 97 percent in favor of keeping out. It is very evident from this that there was almost maximum sentiment in the U.S. against entering the European conflict, either at the beginning when Poland was invaded, or later when Norway and France were likewise invaded. Over the years the percentage was reduced from 97 to approximately 85 percent and remained the same right up to the attack on Pearl Harbor.

FDR was then surrounded by a group of appointees who were interventionists; many were communist apologists. Among them was Averell Harriman, who, like Assistant Secretary of State Acheson, realized after the barn door was open that Stalin and communism were bitter enemies of freedom and the United States.

Roosevelt boasted that "Harry Hopkins and Uncle Joe Stalin got along like a house on fire. They have become buddies." Hopkins never tired of plugging for his friend Stalin. He said it was ridiculous to think of Stalin as a communist. He was a Russian nationalist.

Sidney Hillman took the same distorted view of Stalin and so did Harold Ickes. Hopkins and Hillman, in addition to former Ambassador Joseph Davies, were deceived by Stalin and passed on their illusions to Roosevelt, who assured visitors that Stalin was not a communist at all, just a Russian patriot.

Henry Wallace, when vice-president, was an outspoken communist-appeaser and even talked about encouraging a people's revolution in Europe to advance the cause of the common man. When Truman became president, Wallace wrote him a letter which was released to the press, stating his views on what the American policy on Russia should be. He was so proRussian that he urged yielding on every issue. President Truman, who had little use for communism, requested his resignation soon afterwards.

I was amazed in reading a biography entitled *Roosevelt, the Soldier of Freedom,* by Professor James MacGregor Burns, in which I was mentioned fifteen times, that I was Roosevelt's worst enemy. This was news to me as I always thought that Huey Long, General Charles de Gaulle, or Alfred E. Smith held that honor. I thought I was further down the list, behind Senators Burton Wheeler, Tydings, Robert Reynolds, Pat McCarran, Bennett Clark, David Walsh, and Congressman Martin Dies. These were all Democrats but I am willing to accept the laurel wreath as the top Republican, followed by Robert Moses of the Triborough Bridge Authority, Robert Taft, Thomas E. Dewey, Senator Nye, Colonel McCormick, Colonel Lindbergh, Joseph Martin, and Bruce Barton, of the political firm of Martin, Barton and Fish.

I do not blame FDR for hating me; not only did I come

from his own congressional district, where I remained undefeated, but I was constantly criticizing both his socialistic domestic policies and war-provoking foreign policies, in the House and over the major radio networks. I did not mince words, but they were based on the pending issues, not on personalities or sentiment. I can truthfully say that I never hated FDR, but I did feel very strongly about some of his socialistic and pro-war measures. I believe he feared that I might become chairman of the Rules Committee, where I would have been in a position to have blocked his path to socialism and his road to war and, if warranted on Constitutional grounds, to have introduced impeachment proceedings. The truth is that the entire foreign policy of the President — from the time of the transfer of fifty destroyers to Britain, the stationing of troops in Iceland, and his shoot-at-sight order — proceeded without the consent of the Congress. FDR's foreign policy was a policy of deceit; it double-crossed the American people. As a candidate for reelection to a third term, he repeatedly assured the voters of his devotion to the preservation of peace. His peace pledge in Boston was a vivid example of his hypocrisy and trickery towards the American people while soliciting their votes.

It is difficult now to reconcile Roosevelt's policies with his message on the State of the Union to the Congress on January 6, 1941. He said we were "committed . . . for our own security which will never permit us to acquiesce in a peace dictated by aggressors and sponsored by appeasers. *We know that enduring peace cannot be bought at the cost of other people's freedom."* (Author's italics.)

Looking back on the destruction of the freedom of Poland, Czechoslovakia, Hungary, the Balkans, and the Baltic states, the peace was a travesty on freedom everywhere. It is also difficult to understand FDR's statement to Congress about not acquiescing in a peace with which we were not involved. We were not then even committed to go to war. Congress had never voted for it.

The following is part of my testimony on February 15, 1938, before the Naval Affairs Committee of the House of Representatives, headed by the Honorable Carl Vincent, an able and respected Democrat. This was eighteen months before the outbreak of World War II.

MR. FISH: I am convinced that the American people are absolutely opposed, except for the 10 percent internationalists, to President Roosevelt's request for power to establish blockades, sanctions, embargoes, concerted actions, or to determine the aggressor nation. They all amount to justifiable causes for war, in policing and quarantining other nations by coercion and force.

These acts of aggression have been going on for several hundred years. Great Britain seized half the world, France seized large colonies, and Italy and other nations have, including Russia and Germany, and we have not interfered.

I am putting in the record the recent speech of former President Herbert Hoover who stated it a little more strongly, and my reply in support of his speech: Hon. Herbert Hoover, Palo Alto, Calif., Telegram, January 17, 1938: As ranking Republican member, House

Foreign Affairs Committee, commend your peace program. Am inserting it in the Congressional Record. Glad to know you do not endorse the internationalism of Henry L. Stimson who agrees with FDR in concerted action through embargoes and armed force in quarantining other nations. The American people are for peace, not war. Hamilton Fish.

V

THE MARCH TO WAR

The internationalists' and interventionists' cauldron
began to seethe and bubble in the United States two
years before the outbreak of World War II. The ingredients which Macbeth's witches used for their hell's
broth were not more terrible or infernal than those
thrown into the pre-war brew by President Roosevelt
and his belligerent pro-war cabinet. What were those
ingredients? Quarantining the aggressor nations with
the lives of American boys, policing the world with
blood and treasure, proclaiming war embargoes,
undermining our traditional neutrality and peace position for so-called collective security around the world
— one-worldism, and demands by the President for
unlimited power and money from Congress to involve
us in war without the necessity of a declaration of war.

This was the brew that enabled FDR to meddle and
interfere with the foreign policies of European and
Asian nations and to involve us in their age-old con-
flicts. Roosevelt was a determined internationalist and
interventionist. He had been a candidate for vice-president on the Democratic ticket in 1920 on a rigid inter-

nationalist pro-League of Nations platform. FDR had a secret obsession about using the high office of the presidency to influence, cajole, threaten, and directly or indirectly interfere with the foreign policies of England, France, and Poland. He sought to persuade Poland to refuse to negotiate for the restoration of Danzig, whose population was 90 percent German, to the Third Reich, until it was too late. Not satisfied with direct meddling, he indulged in provocative name-calling against the heads of totalitarian nations such as Italy, Germany, and later Japan, but never against Soviet Russia or Joseph Stalin. His language and epithets, and those of Secretary Ickes, were so inflammatory that he automatically ruled himself out as a potential peacemaker. That did not bother him because war was his objective and to act as a peacemaker was not what he had in mind. His constant thought, from September 1, 1939, to December 7, 1941, was to maneuver the United States into war.

Once World War II had begun, FDR was determined to involve us in it. Why? 1) To keep promises and implied promises; 2) to relieve a tragic unemployment situation — 13 million unemployed after six years of New Deal policies and failures; 3) desire as an internationalist to intervene in the actual conduct of the war; 4) lust for power and a place in history as a war president; 5) the creation of the United Nations with himself as the de facto ruler or co-leader with Stalin.

Jesse H. Jones was a member of Roosevelt's cabinet as Secretary of Commerce, a Democrat who also headed the Reconstruction Finance Corporation. In his book, *Fifty Billion Dollars*, he refers to Roosevelt as the "total politician." He helps to clarify FDR's desire and determination to get into war: "Regardless of his oft-repeated statement, 'I hate war,' he was eager to get into the fighting, since that would insure a third term. A third term would have gratified his two highest ambitions — to get into the war, and his vanity to be re-elected as the first third-term President." He accomplished both by assuming the character of Doctor Jekyll and Mr. Hyde, posing as the peace candidate while he and his cabinet were doing everything in their power to maneuver the American people into war against their will.

There is an inexorable law greater than man-made laws. It is that truth will prevail. The minions of truth are stirring in the womb of history. History must uphold the realities of truth so that it may light the darkness.

FDR's pro-war policy was like the bird who feigns to have a broken wing in order to decoy the enemy from destroying its nest and fledglings. He publicly pursued a policy of guile and subterfuge. He proclaimed his love of peace and hatred of war, but war was in his mind.

"War was in his heart: his words were softer than oil, yet were they drawn swords" (Psalms 55:4).

If Roosevelt had refrained from meddling in the European situation by encouraging England and France to believe that we would fight their battles, they would have reached an agreement by peaceful means to settle the Danzig issue, avoided the disastrous war, and protected their own colonial interests. The American people, regardless of their antipathy to Nazism, were opposed to sending their sons to fight over the possession of Memel or Danzig, or other territories seized under the Versailles Treaty, or to be slaughtered in defense of communism and Soviet Russia, or to defend French and British colonial empires. With Soviet Russia the most despotic and dictatorial nation in existence allied to Great Britain and France, a European war could not be fought for freedom and democracy, but for world power and the support of vast colonial empires.

As far back as April 21, 1939, four months before the outbreak of the war, the American people began to realize that the Roosevelt administration was openly pro-war. It stood for internationalism, intervention, collective security, secret diplomacy, military alliances, and against our traditional American foreign policy of neutrality, nonintervention and peace. FDR and New Deal spokesmen, including members of the cabinet, stirred up war hysteria into a veritable frenzy. The New Deal propaganda machine worked overtime to prepare and condition the minds of our people for war, and once again to send our youth to foreign battlefields.

What was behind the far-reaching and continuous campaign of hate emanating from the White House and daily discovering a new crisis? One word from the President would have stopped the hysteria and talk of war. But no such word came. Instead there was a steady flow of alarming and provocative statements that added fuel to the flames of war.

On April 11, 1939, President Roosevelt endorsed an editorial in the *Washington Post* that stated, "If war broke out in Europe, our participation in it would be a virtual necessity." The facilities of the President and the New Deal administration to disseminate war propaganda and hysteria, to prepare the youth of America for another bloodbath in Europe, was so enormous that a national organization to counteract these provocative and dangerous policies, the America First Committee, was formed to keep America out of foreign wars.

"Would that mine enemy write a book," is an old saying, but it is even worse to have a friend write a book like *Roosevelt and Hopkins: An Intimate History*. The author, Robert E. Sherwood, proves beyond a shadow of a doubt that what the noninterventionists (whom Sherwood always called "isolationists") were claiming was correct — that FDR was a militant, pro-war interventionist. From the time of his quarantine speech of October 5, 1937, up to and after the beginning of World War II on September 3, 1939, his foreign policy was to meddle in the bloody game of European power politics.

The great rank and file of the American people had been appalled by the casualties and huge costs of World War I. After the victory, largely won by United States troops, we asked for nothing and got exactly what we asked for. No thanks, no war booty, no reparations, nothing at all except to be called Uncle Shylock. Britain and France did not repay their war debts to us, even the interest. An indignant President Calvin Coolidge remarked, "They hired the money, didn't they?" Is there any wonder that most Americans were in favor of keeping out of European wars? They were rightly noninterventionists in war, not the isolationists depicted by Mr. Sherwood, one of FDR's ablest ghost writers.

Sherwood states in his book that FDR realized the strong antiwar sentiment in the country and did not dare to meet it head on. Consequently, he was careful from the beginning to avoid getting too far out on a pro-war limb where there could be no reconsideration. Instead FDR tried in every way to alarm the nation through propaganda that German planes would bomb Denver and that German panzer divisions would cross over from Africa to Brazil on their way to attack New York. The hysteria unleashed by the vast government propaganda sources alarmed the people without any justification. It was an abominable attempt to excite peace-loving Americans with ghost stories of bombing by Nazi airplanes and attacks by panzer divisions. (In Brazil they would be much farther away from the United States than from Germany and could not have got through the impassable swamps and forests of northern Brazil.) We learn from Sherwood that FDR was a cloak-and-dagger internationalist who used extraofficial channels. One was Lord Beaverbrook, and once the war had broken out, there was a still partially unpublished historic correspondence of 1,700 messages with Winston Churchill; some of the most critical may never see the light of day.

My ancestors came to America from England 349 years ago to get away from the ceaseless religious and civil wars of Europe, and so did the ancestors of most other Americans. However, Field Marshall Harry Hopkins, Secretary Ickes, Morgenthau, Harriman, Henry Wallace and President Roosevelt, most of whom were invincible in peace, but invisible in war, were determined to send our sons back into the ceaseless wars of Europe and Asia. I have much more respect for Secretaries Stimson and Knox, two leading red-hot interventionists and warmakers, because they had served in the armed forces of the United States in the previous war.

In speaking about FDR's pro-war propaganda, no one knew more about it than his Secretary of the Navy, Frank Knox, who, referring to the effectiveness of New Deal propaganda, said, "This is a political propaganda machine the like of which this country has never seen." It went into high gear when Knox and Stimson joined the cabinet — not to support the New Deal, which both disapproved of, but to aid a massive, gigantic continuous pro-war propaganda machine not even limited to the United States.

When the people of the U.S. began to take sides over going in or keeping out of World War II, the administration started a totally false and fictitious creation of word images. The image makers coined the word "isolationist," purposely designed as a disparaging word, to the delight of the warmakers, interventionists, and oneworlders. Ninety percent of the forefathers of the American people migrated from foreign lands in order to avoid the hardships, privations, and wars of the Old World. Actually, there was no such animal as an isolationist — that is, a person who is opposed to dealing with, trading, and maintaining diplomatic relations with other countries. Instead, the overwhelming majority of Americans were noninterventionists. Remembering the disillusionments of World War I, they were openly opposed to our entrance into World War II unless we were attacked.

The new epithets — "obstructionists," "Nazis," "Fascists," "ostriches," "copperheads," and "isolationists" — were of no avail, because the American people could not be moved from their honest convictions that we should keep out of the bloody feuds and power politics of Europe.

The late President John F. Kennedy said at Yale University on June 11, 1962: "The greatest enemy of the truth is very often not the lie — deliberate, contrived and dishonest — but the myth — persistent, persuasive and unrealistic."

Most historical interpretations contain polemics and controversy. The main objective of the historian is to dispel with truth the innuendos, half-truths and misrepresentations that have been perpetuated over the years on an unsuspecting and uninformed public.

On the walls of Hunter College, New York City, engraved in large letters is the following quotation from Ralph Waldo Emerson: "We are of different opinions at different hours, but we always may be said to be at heart on the side of truth."

The following is part of a speech I made over the National Broadcasting Company's radio network. It was about the only way to reach the American people.

> The interventionists and pro-war press of the east and south would not carry a line, if they could help it, giving the views of an overwhelming majority of our people who want to stay out of war unless attacked. The American people have long since seen through the interventionism of the eastern press, columnists and pro-war commentators, and the moving picture industry, to drive them into the war against their will. This inspired propaganda left the American people cold, even in the summertime.

Every American has a right to his or her views on the vital issue of war or peace, and to express them openly and freely. The 15 percent who are for participation in war, represented by the Fight for Freedom Committee, a misnomer after Yalta, had an absolute right to urge an immediate declaration of war without being called names or being denounced as placing the interest of the British Empire before that of America.

I agreed with Senator Pepper that if we entered the war it might last five years and cost 100 billion dollars a year. I do not believe that many American mothers wanted their sons to die in darkest Africa, in the vastness of China, fight for Soviet Russia, or to make Europe safe for communism. On the other hand, every American mother would have been willing to give the life of her son in the defense of the United States and the American continent.

President Roosevelt in a letter to the Young Democratic Clubs of America urged all isolationists to leave the Democratic party. Thomas Jefferson, the founder of the party, would turn in his grave. Jefferson was the leading noninterventionist of American history. He repeatedly urged that we keep out of the eternal wars of Europe. Jefferson founded the Democratic party and Franklin D. Roosevelt unfounded, or dumbfounded, Jefferson. President Roosevelt wanted to purge and read out of the Democratic party such able and courageous senators as Wheeler of Montana, Clark of Missouri, Clark of Idaho, Walsh of Massachusetts, McCarran of Nevada, Reynolds of North Carolina, and even Senator LaFollette, a progressive from Wisconsin, for seeking to keep America out of war unless attacked.

If FDR had succeeded in reading the noninterventionists out of the Democratic party north of the

Mason-Dixon line, he would have had nothing left but the office holders of the party and the Fight for Freedom Committee, somewhat misnamed after the U.S.S.R. entered the war and more so after the Yalta betrayal.

Roosevelt's statement injected reckless partisanship into the greatest single issue before the American people, that of our involvement in foreign wars. Noninterventionists in both the Democratic and Republican parties representing most of the American people were strongly for national defense. The difference is that the noninterventionists wanted to protect and safeguard the United States and the American continent, and not go out looking for war all over the world.

The American people should decide their own destiny within the confines of the Constitution. If FDR had sent a war declaration to the Congress it would have been defeated by a vote of four to one. Every American is in favor of making the United States invincible on land, sea, and in the air, so that we can meet and defeat any attack by any group of aggressor nations upon us or South America. Our navy, the largest and finest in the world, and many times greater than the German navy, guaranteed that there could be no successful attack made upon us. Within a few years our two-ocean navy will be completed. And within a year, our army will be equipped with artillery, tanks, airplanes, and antitank and anti-aircraft guns sufficient to repel any possible invasion of this continent.

This sums up in a nutshell the vast anti-war sentiment that prevailed in the U.S. from the outset of the war in Europe. Now, what about the 15 percent of the population who were pro-war advocates? Where did they come from?

They were a small, but very well and heavily financed group, representing the international bankers, and newspapers in the big northeastern cities, such as the *New York Times,* the *New York Herald Tribune* (Republican), the *Washington Post,* the *Baltimore Sun,* the *Boston Globe,* and most of the Philadelphia papers. They were a tremendous source of constant interventionist propaganda. In addition, in the Northeast, well-to-do socialite families, through European marriages or business associations, were belligerently pro-British or pro-French. They were few in number but vociferous, rich, and powerful. Then there was a so-called intellectual element which was distinctly pro-war, such as university presidents Conant of Harvard, Seymour of Yale, Nicholas Murray Butler of Columbia, and Dodd of Princeton.

These pro-war groups were small but powerful in financial circles, in the press, and on the radio. But by far the most important and effective pro-war sentiment came from the Southern states. There was still in the South a considerable latent sympathy and goodwill for the British because of its moral support of the Confederate States during the Civil War. But there were other ties to Britain among the pro-war Southerners. Many were of British origin and, even more important, were dyed-in-the wool Democrats.

If it had not been for the hard-core Democrats from the South in the House and in the Senate, most of FDR's step-by-step unneutral and pro-war measures would have been scrapped in Congress. The South was by far the most warlike section of the nation and naturally was inclined to follow a Democratic president. Only one senator from the South, Robert Reynolds from North Carolina, was an active noninterventionist. However, he was fearless, outspoken, and held an important position as chairman of the Military Affairs Committee in the Senate. He also had the courage of his convictions, and FDR could not intimidate him.

The Southern members of Congress can justly claim major responsibility for the passage of Roosevelt's prowar measures and for the steps toward American involvement in war. But in fairness to them, probably not more than 20 percent would have voted for a *declaration* of war unless there was a definite attack on the United States or its armed forces.

Speaker Sam Rayburn, a likeable and able Democrat from Texas, was as internationalist and interventionist as FDR but never served a day in our armed forces; neither did Harry L. Hopkins, the alter ego of FDR, Sidney Hillman, the left-wing labor leader, Vice-President Henry A. Wallace, Clifton Woodrum, and others in the House. But the Republican party had such men, too: Thomas E. Dewey and Nelson A. Rockefeller, for example, both of whose presidential ambitions were ruined by the votes of the American war veterans.

The Northern and Western Democrats were fairly solid for my volunteer amendment to the draft bill, which passed the House by a vote of 207 to 200. Later on in the final extension of the draft bill, it was adopted by a vote of 211 to 210, with the Southerners voting for it.

There is a definite reason for describing the anti-war

sentiment in the nation and the different situation in the Congress which was two-thirds Democratic in both the House and the Senate. Above and beyond the Congress stood the "great white father" and Harry Hopkins, with his spend-tax-and-elect program that had been so helpful in electing Democrats to Congress. It is not surprising that those Democratic members of the House who stood for election every two years were willing to follow the President on all measures allegedly short of war.

One of the most courageous and outspoken Democrats, who opposed every step towards war in the House, was Louis Ludlow of Indiana. He introduced a referendum war measure which came very near to winning a majority of the votes in the House. It took all the power of the administration to prevent its passage.

Who were the main opponents to war in the United States? The American Federation of Labor headed by William Greene; John L. Lewis, head of the United Mine Workers; farm organizations; the church elements, Catholic, Methodist, Baptist, Lutheran, and many others; a majority of our women; the America First Committee and other peace organizations; Norman Thomas; many liberals; most of the large German and Italian population; and many disillusioned veterans who served with distinction in World War I, such as General Robert Wood, Theodore Roosevelt, Jr., and Hanford McNeider, later national commander of the American Legion.

All of these groups combined with the rank and file of the American people, who preferred peace to war.

On June 29, 1941, former President Herbert Hoover

exposed the entrance of Soviet Russia into the war as undermining the interventionists' pleas that the United States "should join the conflict to preserve Democratic principles and ideals," as Stalinist Russia was "one of the bloodiest tyrannies and terrors ever created in human history."

Hoover then predicted what has since become true — if we did join the war and won, "then we have won for Stalin the grip of Communism on Russia and more opportunity for it to expand over the world."

Senator Bennett Clark (D. Mo.) pointed out that Stalin was "as bloody handed" as Hitler, and the United States should let these bloody dictators destroy themselves.

Senator Harry Truman, later President, denounced both dictators and said: "If Russia were winning, help should be given to Germany and if Germany were winning, help should be given to Russia."

Looking back on history, Truman showed great foresight. Senator Robert M. La Follette of Wisconsin, with whom I debated in numerous cities across the nation, also had the same views as Senator Truman. "The American people will be told to forget the purges in Russia by the OGPU, the confiscation of property, persecution of religion, the invasion of Finland and the vulture role Stalin played by seizing half of prostrate Poland, all of Latvia, Estonia and Lithuania." La Follette also foresaw the manace to freedom from Soviet communism.

VI

INTERVIEW WITH THE
GERMAN FOREIGN MINISTER
JOACHIM VON RIBBENTROP,
AUGUST 14, 1939

This is an account of my exclusive interview with Joachim von Ribbentrop, the German Nazi foreign minister at his mountain villa near Salzburg, Austria, two weeks before the outbreak of World War II. It was prepared and written from copious notes taken at the time, and is now presented to the American people and to all others interested in truth and history.

The interview took place 44 years ago. Certainly the facts can now be told without arousing political animosity between nations. It might even serve to scotch misleading rumors and absurd implications that may have existed at the time. Herr von Ribbentrop was sentenced many years ago by the Nuremberg Court and hanged. I went to Salzburg at the invitation of the German foreign minister in my official capacity as president of the American delegation to the Interparliamentary Union. I was on my way to the annual convention to be held at Oslo, Norway, August 15-19, 1939.

The American delegation was composed of twenty-four members of the House of Representatives, equally divided between the two parties, and four U.S. senators. Two of these, Senator Theodore Francis Greene and Senator Alexander Wiley, later served with distinction as chairmen of the Senate Foreign Relations Committee.

For a number of years, Senator Alben W. Barkley, later vice-president of the United States, had been elected as president of the American delegation to the Interparliamentary Union by the members of the House and Senate. In the early part of 1939, there was a good deal of war talk and fear that President Roosevelt would involve us directly or indirectly in another European war. A majority of the Congress, both Republicans and Democrats, were in favor of keeping out of foreign wars unless attacked. My views as ranking Republican member of the House Foreign Affairs Committee were well known in Congress and throughout the nation.

I was openly opposed to having the U.S. dragged into the ancient European blood feuds and balance-of-power politics, and so were approximately 90 percent of the American people at that time. A number of my friends in Congress asked me if I would serve as president of the Interparliamentary Union if there were enough votes to defeat Senator Barkley. I agreed, and to my surprise I was elected by a two-to-one margin.

The result was an even greater surprise to Senator Barkley, who had for years been the supreme autocrat of the Interparliamentary Union and who was considered politically unbeatable. Hitherto, Barkley had distributed the $10,000 appropriated by Congress each year to seven or eight senators, mostly Democrats, and to two or three representatives. In view of the fact that my election over Senator Barkley was almost revolutionary, I decided to fill the entire American quota of twenty-eight members, which I proceeded to do by appointing twelve Republicans and an equal number of Democrats from the House, and two Democrats and two Republicans from the Senate. The $10,000 appropriation, at $500 per member, took care of twenty members and the others agreed to pay their own expenses. Then I received a contribution of $3,000 from Bernard Baruch, which provided $500 for most of the others. This was the first time that the full American quota had been appointed and the first time that the membership had represented both parties equally.

For several years I had realized the crucial and delicate balance of the scales in Europe between war and peace, and I had determined, both in Congress and as president of the American delegation, to exert my utmost influence toward the preservation of peace, as opposed to an utterly ruinous European world war. I remember telling or warning von Ribbentrop that no matter which nation won, if war broke out, every European nation engaged in it would lose lives, and endure destruction and bankruptcy. It did not take much of a prophet to foresee that eventuality. At no time did I receive any cooperation from President Roosevelt; he was, I am reliably informed, very much annoyed at my election as head of the delegation, and likewise by my efforts at Oslo to settle the Danzig issue by peaceful means instead of by another European bloodbath.

After Congress adjourned at the end of July, 1939, I went by boat to Ireland where I met President De Valera at his office in Dublin. He was a tall, intelligent, kindly, and outspoken public official. He stated without reservations that if the European war broke out and England were involved, Ireland would remain neutral but would sell food and other products to England.

From Dublin I flew to London to keep a Saturday afternoon appointment with Lord Halifax, the British foreign minister at his office. He later became the British ambassador to Washington. He was very tall, charming, and able — a cultured gentleman and statesman. He looked something like Abraham Lincoln. He was outspokenly against war with Germany and told me that the Nazi government had proposed to limit its army to 300,000, provided France would also, and he deplored France's refusal to agree. He felt, as I did, that another European war would be ruinous and that every possible constructive effort should be made to avoid it.

I then flew to Paris to meet my wife and children who had preceded me there by boat from the United States. I met the French foreign minister Georges Bonnet by appointment. I thought him a talented and experienced diplomat but inclined to the defeatist attitude that war was inevitable and would break out within a few weeks. Obviously he did not want France to become involved in a war with Germany, but from reports I received he was being pressured into it by certain powerful public figures both in the United States and Great Britain. He realized that France was not sufficiently prepared in air power and lacked enough armored tanks.

Also while in Paris, I met the good-looking young French air minister, Guy LaChambre at a small dinner party given by our amiable and astute Ambassador William C. Bullitt, at his exquisite chateau at Chantilly near Paris. He was only thirty-seven but had served in the French army in World War I and had been decorated for gallantry. He was then in somewhat the same position in France as Goering was in Germany. He had revived and reorganized the French air force and was in the process of building it up into a powerful weapon for the defense of France. Had he had another year, he could have succeeded. I talked with him for an hour after dinner, and he told me in a calm and deliberate manner that France was preparing for any eventuality and that war would probably break out by August 24. I argued as best I could, pointing out that in modern wars all nations lost, including the victor, and that it was not too late to reach a peaceful agreement with Germany. I told him I expected to see von Ribbentrop in a few days and asked him if what he had told me was confidential and he answered most emphatically, "No." The French air minister evidently greatly underestimated the size and power of the German air force, as later events proved.

During the first week of August while I was staying at the Roblin Hotel in Paris with my family, I received a telephone call from a German friend of mine, Mr. Sallett in Berlin, asking me if I would like to meet the German foreign minister, von Ribbentrop. I told him I would be glad to stop off on my way to Norway for the interparliamentary convention. I knew of no reason then (nor know of any now) why I shouldn't have met the German foreign minister. In fact, I felt it my duty as head of the American congressional group to meet von Ribbentrop and obtain all available information about the intention or plans of the German government as it affected the peace of Europe and the world. I had already seen Lord Halifax, the British foreign minister, in London, and Georges Bonnet, the French foreign minister, and Guy LaChambre, the French air minister, in Paris. I suggested Monday, August 14th at Salzburg, the day before the Oslo Conference.

Herr Richard Sallett, an official of the German foreign office and a graduate of Harvard University, whom I had known in America, entertained me in Berlin. I went with him to the foreign office where I met Baron Weizbaecker, who ranked next to von Ribbentrop. He was, I believe, formerly in the naval service, and spoke English well. His only son was killed three weeks later while serving as an officer in the Polish campaign. He apparently was not a Nazi, nor in favor of the invasion of Poland. I arrived with Sallett at Salzburg by train from Berlin on Monday morning, August 14, and was taken straight to the same hotel at which Count Ciano was staying. At breakfast I met von Ribbentrop's personal liaison officer, Colonel Huwell, later an ambassador. He was killed escaping from Hitler's bunker at the end of the war. He informed me that my appointment had been postponed until four o'clock that afternoon as the result of Ciano's visit. This delay aroused my Holland Dutch blood and I informed

prepared, and that if disorders continued in Poland, war was inevitable. I remember he said that "the mechanized German army can crush and overwhelm Poland in two weeks." I laughed at that and said, "You mean two months don't you?" To which he replied, "No, in two weeks," and continued, "We are familiar with every road in Poland from the last war and know Poland as well as the Poles, and the muddy roads of Poland do not frighten us."

Herr von Ribbentrop reiterated that for years Hitler, whom he called the Fuehrer, was animated by racial consideration and belief in the stability of the British Empire. He said he had flown twenty or more times to London with friendly proposals and goodwill messages to the British government from Hitler. For a number of years von Ribbentrop was the German ambassador to London. He referred to Hitler's offer to limit the German army to 300,000, which France had rejected; and to the offer to limit the German navy to one-third the size of the British navy, which was accepted. He went even further and said that Hitler believed that cooperation between England and Germany was essential for the maintenance of peace, and that Hitler had "offered to place fifteen German army divisions and the entire fleet at the disposal of the British government to support her empire in case of war anywhere in the world."

This I did not believe at the time, but it was substantiated years later. He said it was not until the British inaugurated their program of encirclement and guarantee of the status quo of Danzig that Hitler turned from friendship to bitter enmity. Although von Ribbentrop did not use the words, "like a woman scorned," that was the impression I received. He did say that now the Fuehrer "would stop at nothing to destroy the British Empire even to the last German soldier."

I asked von Ribbentrop who wrote the remarkable reply of April 1939 to President Roosevelt's proposal to guarantee the neutrality of certain nations. I thought that he, as the foreign minister, had done so. However, he claimed that he had shown a translation of the proposal to Hitler, who exclaimed on reading it, "This is an act of Providence," and that Hitler had stayed up the entire night working on the answer himself.

Herr von Ribbentrop told me that he (von Ribbentrop) had written to Monsieur Bonnet, the French foreign minister, to the effect that the German Westwall (the Siegfried Line) was completed, invincible, and that the Germans had no quarrel with the French; but if the French insisted on attacking, they would lose a million men and bleed to death. That, he said, was France's responsibility, not his.

It was not my mission to quarrel with the foreign minister; the only dispute I got into was when he tried to convince me that the German army did not lose the last war. I reminded him that I, too, was an officer in that war and that the German soldiers and replacements were either young boys of sixteen or men over forty-five and that Germany was exhausted in manpower and resources and could not have lasted another six months regardless of the revolution at home. He did not press the issue any further.

During the conversation, which lasted over an hour and a half, we drank tea and ate cookies and preserves. My reception throughout was most cordial and courteous. He invited me to go to the opera with Hitler that evening and assured me that if I did, he would arrange for his plane to get me to Oslo by nine the next morning. I declined for several reasons; one, I did not believe it worth the risk of being late in reaching Oslo, and the other political. Looking back, I regret not having met the megalomaniac Hitler at the apex of his power.

Despite Hitler's friendly attitude toward the British, von Ribbentrop was antagonistic.

History has often shown that small things have caused enmity and war between nations. The British aristocracy, despite the fact that von Ribbentrop was ambassador of the German Reich, one of the most powerful governments in Europe, apparently could not overlook the fact that he had been a former champagne salesman. This form of snobbishness was carried to the extent that von Ribbentrop's son was blackballed socially and turned down for Harrow and Eton. This is something that no father, whether ambassador or not, can forget or forgive, and from then on he used his influence against the British wherever possible. It is a sad commentary on diplomacy, but human nature has not changed for thousands of years, and this little family episode was a contributing factor toward World War II.

When the motor car arrived to take me to the airfield, von Ribbentrop politely escorted me to the car. That was the last time I ever saw or heard from him. Ten days later he signed the pact with Stalin for a German-Russian alliance, one week after the Interparliamentary Union failed to adopt my resolution for a 30-day moratorium to settle the Danzig issue by arbitration.

Years later von Ribbentrop was hanged. Just why I do not know; it may have been because he succeeded in making a war alliance with Stalin and Molotov in August 1939, when England and France failed to secure the same kind of treaty. In any case many lawyers have raised the issue of *ex post facto* law at the trials. I do know that von Ribbentrop, condemned at the Nuremberg Trials for alleged crimes knew as most other people did of the terrible communist atrocities, including the murder of 12,000 Polish officers (prisoners), 38,000 of their own officers, and the brutal liquidation of millions of Russian people.

Certainly those Germans directly responsible for atrocities, such as the killing of innocent people in concentration camps or otherwise, should have been held guilty for their barbaric actions. But I have, along with Robert Taft, always doubted the legality of holding a foreign minister and top officers of the army and navy responsible for atrocities over which they had no authority, any more than General Marshall, General Eisenhower, or Secretary of State Cordell Hull should be held responsible for the killing of over 150,000 Germans in the bombing and burning of Dresden, or that President Truman and his advisers should be held responsible for the death of 120,000 Japanese by atomic bombs at Nagasaki and Hiroshima.

Of course individuals should be held responsible for war crimes. But to have Soviet Russia, which invaded Poland two weeks after the Nazi invasion in 1939, participate in the Nuremberg Trials, made the Trials largely a farce and a travesty of justice, if their purpose was to establish a definite standard for wars of aggression, war crimes, or atrocities.

VII

PEACEFUL ARBITRATION
OR WAR?

The subject of this chapter is of such tremendous importance — involving as it does the direct cause of the greatest war in the history of the world, in casualties, destruction, and the loss of freedom — that the full story must be told, without omissions. The magnitude of the issue involved, and the great efforts made by most of the pre-war statesmen to prevent the outbreak of World War II, have an important place in history.

In *The Rise and Fall of the Third Reich* by William L. Shirer, there are at least fifty pages of material outlining the efforts of England, France, Germany, and numerous others, including the Pope, Mussolini, the King of the Belgians and even, at the last minute, President Roosevelt, to prevent such a catastrophe.

Nearly everyone of prominence was anxious to avoid war by having Poland agree to enter into direct negotiations with Germany. There was one stumbling block: Polish Foreign Minister Jozef Beck had previously recognized the German viewpoint, but after he obtained the utterly useless guarantee of British armed protection he did an about-face and took a very strong posi-

tion against negotiation. Danzig had a German population of 90 percent, who voted overwhelmingly in a
referendum to be restored to the German Reich in
accordance with the principles of self-determination.
The German aggressions against Czechoslovakia were
ruthless and impossible to defend, but the desire of
Nazi Germany to negotiate for the return of Danzig
and a Corridor is understandable, and should never
have been permitted by England and France to become
the cause of World War II.

What were the real reasons that delayed, obstructed,
and ultimately prevented direct negotiations between
Germany and Poland for the restoration of Danzig? By
this time England and France, through their top officials, were urging Poland to send emissaries with full
powers to determine the Danzig issue on a peaceful
basis. England and France had both made it very clear
that if Germany invaded Poland, they would declare
war on Germany. However, Prime Minister Chamberlain was exceedingly anxious to head off a catastrophic
war and had even appealed to President Roosevelt
through Ambassador Kennedy to have the President
use his influence.

Hitler was also very anxious to settle the Danzig
issue peacefully to avoid bringing England and France
into the war. He was greatly annoyed by the Polish
refusal even to consider any concessions on Danzig or
to appoint plenipotentiaries to discuss them. He finally
ordered an invasion of Poland on August 24, but at the
last minute canceled it because of pleas from various
quarters.

The frantic pleadings of both France and England

and messages from the Pope, the King of the Belgians, and the President of the United States, at the eleventh hour, finally induced the Poles to authorize their ambassador in Berlin, Lipski, to see von Ribbentrop and state that Poland was interested in Germany's proposed terms of negotiations. Von Ribbentrop asked Ambassador Lipski, "Do you come here with powers to negotiate?" and when he admitted he did not, that was the end of the efforts to preserve the peace.

The ultimate blame rests on Hitler for forcing the issue by not having the patience to wait another few days, as it was evident that the pressure from all sources would have compelled Poland to enter negotiations. Poland was also to blame for its refusal to even consider concessions regarding Danzig, the final liquidation of the Versailles Treaty. It was especially heartrending in view of the fact that Hitler had made a nonaggression pact with Russia only six days before, and obviously Russia would now be on the side of Germany.

It is almost unbelievable that Foreign Minister Beck and the other high officials of Poland could have been so completely deceived about the actual military situation, when confronted by Germany with the finest army in Europe on the west, and the vast Russian army on the eastern border. Words almost fail to describe such an awesome military situation.

England had only two or three divisions available at that time and could not even provide a pop gun or a fire cracker to help Poland militarily. In fairness to England and France, they did not force the war on Poland. They did everything within their diplomatic power to persuade Poland to enter into negotiations for the restoration of Danzig. This would have in no way reflected on the honor of Poland, as Danzig was a German city and Germany agreed, if it were restored, to sign a treaty to guarantee the independence and integrity of Poland.

The negative reaction of Poland in view of the military situation is almost beyond comprehension. It was a futile, tragic policy on the part of her top political and military leaders, especially as the Polish people were far more hostile to the Communist regime at Moscow than they were to the Nazi regime in Berlin.

Marshall Pilsudski was one of the greatest heroes and statesmen in the history of Poland. Had he been alive, he would have arranged to submit the Danzig issue to arbitration with Germany and would have secured a guarantee from Germany for the independence and integrity of Poland. It is not that Marshall Pilsudski was partial to Nazi Germany, but he knew Soviet Russia and feared and hated communism. Unfortunately for Poland, he died five years before the outbreak of World War II. He was such a forceful character and great military leader that he would have been respected even by Hitler. I have spoken to numerous Polish exiles and they invariably agree that if Marshall Pilsudski had been alive, the Danzig issue could have been arbitrated peacefully and there would have been no invasion of Poland, no World War II, no murder by the communists of 12,000 Polish officers, and no communization of free Poland.

The most vital, controversial pre-war problem in August 1939 was the status of the free city of Danzig. Recovery of that German city was a *sine qua non* to Hitler and to German prestige. Everyone, even the Polish Foreign Minister Beck, recognized, however reluctantly, that Germany had justifiable claims to Danzig. Perhaps that is why Beck sidestepped negotiations until too late.

A few months later, the freedom-loving Baltic nations, with the exception of Finland, were seized by Soviet Russia, and soon after, communized. That was what I had warned against for several years — that the communist vulture, once war broke out, would swoop down and pick up the bloody remains in eastern Europe.

Let us consider what might have happened if Poland had agreed to restore Danzig and a Corridor. Foreign Minister Beck was willing to do so, but pressure from Roosevelt and top Polish generals prevented it until too late.

The return of Danzig to Germany would have deprived the Nazis of an excuse to invade Poland, headed off the Stalin-Hitler nonaggression pact, saved Poland from being a communist state, and would have aborted Hitler's extermination policy of the Jews in Poland.

Hitler would not have made an alliance with Stalin and communism if he could have avoided it. The net result was that Chamberlain's ill-considered plan played into the hands of the advocates of war and actually checkmated his own aspirations for peace. Lloyd George, as well as many conservatives of vision, foresaw the trap, that this commitment to Poland would inevitably involve England in war, regardless of the consequences to British vital interests. But why could not World War II have been avoided and millions of the finest youth of Europe saved from death and mutilation, by civilized methods of mediation over Danzig? With the Danzig issue settled, that reason for World War II, at least, would have been eliminated.

Hitler and Stalin, Nazis and Communists, would certainly sooner or later have fought a ruinous and exhausting war against each other. The people of Europe, preserved from the ever-present threat of war, would have watched while Hitler and Stalin, the two brutal dictators, destroyed each other. If that had happened Britain and France would not have been participants in the war, and peace, freedom, and democracy would have prevailed throughout western Europe.

I am convinced, now more than ever, that World War II in Europe could have been avoided by restoring Danzig and a Corridor to the German Reich. No one, of course, could guarantee Hitler's future actions, but in all probability western Europe would have been saved from a ruinous war, and Hitler and Stalin would have fought to mutual destruction; Poland would have been neutral or possibly allied with Germany against Soviet Russia; and the bestial butchery of six million European Jews by Hitler's orders might thus have been averted.

These are events that might have happened, and if they had, they would have saved Europe from the scourge of war, and America from participation in it. It would probably have prevented the communization of eastern Europe and the growth of the powerful communist world conspiracy that now threatens the peace and freedom of the world. If Hitler had won, he would have had his hands full in eastern Europe and Russia during his lifetime. Because of his numerous enemies, this bigoted and cruel dictator's chances for a long life would have been very slim.

The German contention was that, if there had been no British blank check, Hitler could have contrived a peaceful solution to the Polish Danzig problem, provided England did not interfere. On March 21, 1939, von Ribbentrop told the Polish ambassador, Lipski, in Berlin that he hoped Danzig would be restored to the Reich, with a Polish Corridor for access.

But on May 5, 1939, after the British guarantee in a memorandum, the Polish government refused von Ribbentrop's suggestion and the fat was in the fire. Almost immediately Hitler declared that the Polish-German declaration of nonaggression agreed to in 1934 was ended; he also abrogated the Anglo-German nonaggression pact and the agreement to limit the size of the German navy.

Most people now admit that it was a legitimate goal of German policy to try to get Danzig returned to the Reich. Unfortunately, the worthless blank-check guarantee stood in the way of the peaceful settlement I tried to accomplish (and almost did) at the Interparliamentary Conference on August 16, 1939, two weeks before war broke out.

The dilatory action of Poland turned out to be the spark that set off World War II. Roosevelt had the opportunity to be the great peacemaker, but by turning down Chamberlain's request and delaying too long, he failed to do anything to prevent the outbreak of World War II.

Illustrating Roosevelt's pre-war dealings with Poland

is a report by Jerzy Potocki, the Polish ambassador to Washington in the 1930s. The report was found among the Polish diplomatic files seized by the Germans at Warsaw and later confirmed by Mr. Potocki, who was then living in South America.

The statement was made after an extensive interview on January 16, 1939, with Ambassador William C. Bullitt, President Roosevelt's key representative in Europe, who was about to return to his post in Paris. It read as follows:

> It is the decided opinion of the president [Roosevelt] that France and Britain must put an end to any sort of compromises with the totalitarian countries. They must not let themselves in for any discussions aiming at any kind of territorial changes. *They have the moral assurance that the United States will leave the policy of isolation and be prepared to intervene actively on the side of Britain and France in case of war.* (Author's italics.)

This is damning evidence of FDR's pre-war interference, promises of intervention, and positive opposition to any peace compromises regarding Danzig. It is proof positive that Roosevelt, from the beginning of 1939, was using his influence with Britain and France "to put an end to any sort of compromises with the totalitarian countries." Further, Bullitt gives definite assurances that the United States was *"prepared to intervene actively on the side of Britain and France in case of war."* (Author's italics)

Bullitt's statement confirms precisely what the American noninterventionists were saying before the outbreak of the European war. It also goes a long way to substantiate the charge that if FDR had not meddled and pressured Britain and France into the war, there would have been no war in Europe, and the Danzig problem would have been solved by peaceful arbitration. Both Prime Minister Chamberlain and Foreign Minister Georges Bonnet have publicly admitted the pressure and influence of Roosevelt to get them into war against Germany.

Ambassador Potocki's statement after his interview with Ambassador Bullitt is just another link in the chain of positive proof that President Roosevelt was exerting, through Bullitt, and directly with Chamberlain, his powerful pro-war influence. It is the first time in American history that a president of the United States intervened directly in European politics, and to promote war, not peace.

After graduating *cum laude* with a degree in history and government, I was offered an appointment as instructor in history at Harvard, which to this day I am sorry I did not accept. However, I did serve on the Committee on Foreign Affairs in Congress for twenty-five years and have generally kept up with the diplomatic history of our country. I know of no instance in which a president of the United States sought to provoke a war in Europe through ambassadorial and other channels. All of our presidents have stood for peace as a permanent policy, and none had ever used his influence to incite or promote war before. FDR's efforts to encourage a war against the Axis powers in Europe are made clear by Bullitt's activities and statements, the letter from Georges Bonnet, and a similar statement by

Prime Minister Chamberlain to Ambassador Kennedy, repeated to Secretary of the Navy James Forrestal and quoted in his diary. The article by Pearson and Allen quoted in chapter 5 also shows how President Roosevelt helped push Chamberlain into war with Germany. All these statements prove FDR exerted his influence to urge England, France, and Poland to go to war with Hitler.

Looking back, it is a stark tragedy that the fate of Poland and of all eastern Europe had to be sacrificed over the small city of Danzig. Most Americans had never heard of Danzig. World War II was an unnecessary and unwanted war, the most destructive and ruinous in all history — the end of freedom for over 100 million Europeans, not only in Poland, Czechoslovakia, and Hungary but in the Baltic and Balkan nations and eastern Germany.

Lord Lothian, British ambassador to Washington during the War, said in a speech at Chatham House on June 29, 1937: "Now if the principle of self-determination were applied on behalf of Germany in the way in which it was applied against them, it would mean the reentry of Austria into Germany, the Union of the Sudeten Deutsch, Danzig, and probably Memel with Germany, and certain adjustments with Poland in Silesia and the Corridor." Lord Lothian, a highly intelligent, well-informed, patriotic Englishman, made this statement more than two years before the Danzig crisis.

Wars are made by overt acts, acts of omission, or by dilatory tactics. The catastrophe of World War II resulted partially from the dilatory tactics of Col. Józef Beck, foreign minister of Poland, who delayed until it was too late. He refused to comply with the request of the British foreign minister, Lord Halifax, and the British ambassador in Berlin, Sir Nevile Henderson, supported by the French ambassador at Berlin and French Foreign Minister Bonnet, urging that the Polish government negotiate directly with Germany over the restoration of Danzig. Ambassador Henderson stated openly that the German proposals were fair and reasonable. Presumably Mr. Beck did not realize the seriousness of the situation and took upon himself the responsibility of delaying direct negotiations until it was too late to stop the war.

The New York *Daily News* said editorially in June 1940:

> The French catastrophe is a part of one of the great tragic ironies of history, as we see it. Hitler said in *Mein Kampf* that he wanted to go east into Russia. The Ukraine looked to him like the ideal place for Germans to colonize and build up a farming and industrial civilization.
>
> Hitler devoted pages in the same book to kind words about the British, how he considered them the same kind of people as the Germans, what fierce fighters the British were in an emergency, and how Germany's best single bet would always be an alliance with England.
>
> *Mein Kampf* contains some harsh words about France but by building the Westwall, Hitler indicated that he didn't want a war with France — but what he still wanted last August was to go east. The allies wouldn't let him go east. They insisted that he come west. He has come west, with a vengeance.

How true! The *News* editorial was a breath of truth and prophecy in the midst of the hysteria of the war era. Who changed Hitler's mind? Who stopped him from going east? Who compelled him to come west, with disastrous results?

Roosevelt, Bullitt, Churchill, Eden, Vansittart, Amory, Duff Cooper, Daladier, Col. Józef Beck, Marshall Smigly Rydz, and strangely, Neville Chamberlain, Prime Minister of Britain, who desperately sought and wanted peace with Germany but was forced by FDR and the British pro-war element to guarantee Poland support against German aggression.

I was in Danzig the day before the German invasion of Poland, on my way back from a trip, after the Oslo conference, to Finland, Estonia, Latvia, and Lithuania. I telephoned our American ambassador to Poland, Anthony Biddle, a longtime personal friend. He immediately invited me to spend a week with him in Warsaw. Nothing could have been more appealing; he was attractive, gay, and charming, and would have been a delightful host. I told him there was nothing I would rather do, but that the war would probably break out within forty-eight hours and there would be no way for me to join my family in Paris except by a long detour through Constantinople, and then by ship. He was most emphatic that there would be no war, but I knew otherwise. He evidently was unaware of Ambassador Bullitt's pro-war activities with the Polish government. Tony Biddle was a popular ambassador and was obviously in no way responsible for urging the Poles to become involved in the war with Germany.

The war broke out within two days. It was an abom-

ination of desolation for free Poland — torn apart by a
Nazi wolf pack on the west and a Communist wolf pack
on the east.

Among my files, I recently found an interesting letter
from former President Herbert Hoover:

THE DRAKE
Chicago

February 11, 1940

My dear Congressman:
Please find enclosed a copy of a section of an
address which I delivered here last evening.
It bears upon the problems with which you are so
earnestly engaged.

With kind regards,
Herbert Hoover

My part tonight is to discuss an immediate task. We
are faced today with a gigantic task of alleviating the
sufferings of the people of Poland. There are destruction and suffering in Poland that I could not adequately
portray even if I wished to do so. Millions of people
must have food; they must have clothing; they must
have shelter. Whatever can be done by public charity
must be done. But before the next harvest, imports of
food from abroad on a large scale must be found. It may
cost as much as $20,000,000. Charity can be of great
aid, but starvation can be prevented only by the cooperation of governments.

With views to securing this cooperation I joined last fall in organizing the Commission for Relief in Poland. Its primary purpose was to serve the people of German-occupied Poland. It has the presidency of Mr. McCormick and the direction of Maurice Pate, both of whom so ably administered the relief of Poland in 1919.

This problem must be understood by you to whom it is so vital. In order for it to succeed the following conditions must be met:

First: Supplies to German-occupied Poland must pass the British blockade. The British must be guaranteed that these supplies are going to the Polish people and not to their enemy.

Second: Any supplies must be transported over German territory and the German authorities must cooperate to give the necessary guarantees.

The Poles had no reason to trust the power-hungry Nazi dictator, but the price they paid as a result of non-cooperation with the British and French governments' request for direct Polish negotiations with Germany regarding Danzig was a ghastly tragedy for the free world. The Communists at Moscow were the only victors.

VIII

THE JEWISH QUESTION

In the early part of 1943, I introduced a resolution in Congress denouncing Hitler for his inhuman racial policies and for killing millions of Jews in gas chambers in Poland and Germany. For some inconceivable reason, the State Department claimed they had no knowledge of the atrocities, thereby preventing adoption of my resolution calling upon all the nations of the world to protest the barbarous liquidation of the Jews. Every nation in Europe knew by that time of the brutal extermination of European Jews, but for some unknown and unexplained reason, FDR's State Department actually opposed my resolution.

Ben Hecht, in his autobiography, said that "President Roosevelt's failure to raise one of his humanitarian fingers to prevent the extermination of the Jews, his many sullen statements about the Jewish situation, and his spiritual anesthesia to the greatest genocide in history" was beyond comprehension. He added, "I was informed by David Niles, FDR's chief secretary and a Jew, that Roosevelt would not make a speech or issue a statement denouncing the German extermination of the Jews."

One has to admire Ben Hecht not only for his courage but for his prescience and foreknowledge of events. He was completing a one-act show entitled "Call the Next Case" in which Franklin Roosevelt was summoned before the bar of history to state what he had done to save the Jews of Europe. The jury trying the case consisted of twelve dead Jews from German crematoriums. Just as Hecht was finishing his script at the Beverly Hills Hotel, he heard the radio announcement that Roosevelt was dead.

In retrospect I have become an admirer of Ben Hecht because he had the vision, foresight, and the courage to insist that President Roosevelt make a definite moral appeal to world humanity and to all nations, neutral and otherwise, to demand that the Nazi government (Hitler) stop its extermination policy or suffer the moral obloquy of the entire world. If such a definitive announcement had been made from the White House, it might well have stopped the megalomanic Hitler, or at least brought home the truth to the German and Polish people, most of whom probably knew little of Hitler's atrocities.

While Six Million Died, a chronicle of American apathy by Arthur D. Morse, says on the first page that "In January 1944, President Roosevelt was shown the startling conclusions of a secret memorandum, its title 'Acquiescence of This Government in the Murder of the Jews'.

"The untold and shocking story behind this report, never before described in full, exposes the appalling apathy and callousness of our government, particularly the State Department, in the face of Nazi genocide."

The following is quoted from page 34 of Morse's book: "While the Allied declaration was being considered, Representative Hamilton Fish, Jr. of New York telephoned the State Department and inquired about reports of mass murder and whether the State Department had any suggestions for thwarting the Nazis. Fish was an isolationist, but he had been moved by a letter to the *New York Times* from Pierre Van Paasen. Van Paasen, a journalist who had observed the Nazis at first hand, had written: 'To be silent in this hour when thousands of unarmed, innocent Jewish human beings are murdered each day, is not only a betrayal of elementary human solidarity, it is tantamount to giving the bloodthirsty Gestapo *carte blanche* to continue and speed its ghastly program of extermination.'

"Fish's call to the State Department was transferred to Reams. When asked about Van Paasen's statement, the man in charge of 'Jewish questions' replied that the matter was under consideration and that the reports of Nazi killings were unconfirmed."

And from page 95: "Among the more than four million Jews in the United States there was of course great apprehension; there was also paralyzing disagreement about what to do. Sporadic rallies were held across the nation. The largest meeting of 1933 occurred at Madison Square Garden in New York. An audience of twenty thousand within the Garden and thirty-five outside heard former Governor Alfred E. Smith and Senator Robert F. Wagner of New York excoriate the Nazis' racist policies.

"The White House maintained a discreet silence,

neither applauding nor criticizing these expressions of public sentiment. But congressional opinion seemed in the main to support the views of Representative Hamilton Fish, Jr., of New York. Fish defended the right of Jewish groups to protest the violence done to Jews in Germany."

Note: I was never an isolationist, but along with 85 percent of the American people I was an noninterventionist regarding foreign wars.

In the British House of Commons, Sydney Silverman, MP from Liverpool, asked Foreign Secretary Anthony Eden whether it was true that the Germans planned to deport all Jews to eastern Europe and put them to death. "Yes, sir," Eden replied. "I regret to have to inform the House that reliable reports have recently reached his Majesty's government regarding the barbarous and inhuman treatment to which the Jews are being subjected in German occupied Europe." In the House of Lords, Sir Herbert Samuels said: "These dreadful events are the outcome of deliberate planned conscious cruelty to human beings. The only events even remotely parallel to this were the Armenian massacres of 50 years ago . . . They aroused the outspoken indignation of the whole of civilized mankind, and they were one of the causes of the downfall of the Turkish empire."

Every nation and government, in the early part of 1943, knew of Hitler's extermination policy. FDR and the State Department should have turned the ruthless searchlight of publicity on the terrible atrocities. An appeal should have called upon all allies and neutral nations to use their official influence with Hitler and the Nazi government to stop the infamous policy of exterminating defenseless racial and religious minorities, a blatant violation of both international law and the laws of humanity.

CONCLUSION

We have seen how a powerful President, able to muster at will an enormous propaganda machine, can convince the public of almost anything. This is particularly true of a stong *liberal* President, who has virtually the whole force of the media behind him.

The cost of World War II — to Americans, Europeans — East and West, Jews, Nationalist Chinese — is still felt today. The ramifications of that War will be with us forever, as it changed the course of history. Much of that responsibility lies at the doorstep of Franklin Roosevelt.

Will we ever learn from the mistakes of our leaders? Abraham Lincoln said: "Tell the American people the truth and the country will be safe."

So I say, listen to those today who tell the truth about yesterday, and perhaps a day of peace will come tomorrow.

APPENDIX

Thank God we have in America a distinguished writer, John Toland, who has used his own time, expense, and great experience, and though hampered by the lack of government documents lost or destroyed, to finally expose the most devastating coverup of how the United States became involved in World War II.

In my own book, *F.D.R.: The Other Side of the Coin —How We Were Tricked Into World War II*, I used truth as my only guide. As leader of the pro-peace, non-interventionist faction in the House of Representatives, I had, in those years, the support of 85 percent of the American people, who were opposed to our entrance into the war, unless we were attacked. I was a member of Congress from Roosevelt's home district for 25 years, until within a few months of his death. In the last ten years, no one has ever dared challenge any part of my FDR book.

Infamy: Pearl Harbor and Its Aftermath by John Toland, is based on documented truth, as was my book. Toland's book has filled the gap in mine that I was never able to stress, as I had no definite proof at the time I wrote. Toland proves beyond a doubt that FDR, Hull, Stimson, Knox (the latter two both Republicans), General Marshall, and Admiral Stark all knew that the Japanese fleet was heading for Pearl Harbor and deliberately agreed not to send any warning to either Admiral Kimmel or General Short. These top officers of our Army and Navy were sacrificed by FDR and the five members of his war cabinet to cover up their own infamous guilt in not informing the commanding officers of the approach of the Japanese fleet.

Ten days before the attack on Pearl Harbor, FDR and Cordell Hull had issued a war ultimatum to Japan to force the Japanese into war. In doing so, the President and the five members of the war cabinet were responsible not only for the deaths of 3,000 young Americans at Hawaii, but for getting us into a World War that resulted in 300,000 killed, 700,000 wounded, and a cost of trillions of dollars.

FDR, in speaking to Congress about the Japanese attack, called it a "Day of Infamy," but that infamy was caused by the men who sent the war ultimatum to Japan.

There is, in history, no way of impeaching high public officials after they have retired, or after their deaths. But if any American leaders deserved to be impeached for their deliberate coverup, trickery, deceit, and lying to the American people between November 26 and December 7, 1941, it is FDR and his war cabinet.

President Nixon was crucified because some minor officials broke into the Democratic headquarters at the Watergate in Washington, D.C., without his knowledge. No one was killed, wounded, or drowned. Yet President Nixon was forced out of office because he tried to protect some of his appointees who knew about this raid. However, FDR, who maneuvered the American people into the greatest and bloodiest war in history, escaped public condemnation and impeachment. By avoiding the responsibility for not warning Admiral Kimmel and General Short of the approach to Pearl Harbor of the Japanese carrier fleet, FDR and his war cabinet not only committed an act infamous and morally shocking, but allowed to be perpetrated one of the greatest travesties of justice in the history of the United States.

Perhaps even more disastrous, and probably still more catastrophic, was FDR's giveaway, while sick and dying, of the fruits of the allied victory to Joseph Stalin, the ruthless and bloody dictator who had by that time killed 20 million of his own people. FDR betrayed the gallantry and victory of our armed forces, who had fought for freedom and democracy, when he turned over 100 million free and independent people living in Eastern Europe to be communized by Stalin.

He also betrayed our friend Chiang Kai-shek by handing over to Stalin most of Manchuria and a number of important harbors in China. As President Roosevelt claimed to Congress that he had made no secret agreements, the facts of his betrayal of China were not known until after his death.

The bloody wars in Korea and Vietnam were both direct legacies of the tragic Yalta conference, in which Stalin was the only victor. As a result of Yalta, the Soviet Union was to become the greatest imperialist nation in the world.

John Toland's book, *Infamy: Pearl Harbor and Its Aftermath*,[1] should be read by every American. I take the liberty here of quoting from chapter 15, wherein, when

[1]Excerps from *Infamy: Pearl Harbor and Its Aftermath*. (New York: Doubleday & Co., 1982) Reprinted by permission of the author.

the final part of the Japanese decoded messages virtually declaring war, reached the Navy Department, . . . "This message alarmed [Admiral] Wilkinson, who wondered aloud if the Philippines and the Pacific Fleet should be alerted. 'Why don't you pick up the phone and call Kimmel?' he suggested to Admiral Stark, at approximately ten forty-five A.M. Stark lifted the receiver, then shook his head and said, in effect, 'No, I think I will call the President.' But the White House switchboard operator reported that the President was busy. Stark put down the telephone and did nothing."

General Marshall finally reached his office at 11:25 A.M. but took almost another hour before his warning message was filed. Stark offered to send it by the navy system, which was fast under pressure. But Marshall said he could not get it out. The Marshall warning did not reach the commanders at Hawaii until hours after the attack.

Toland speaks of Lawrence Stafford who "exhausted after two months work and almost sleepless nights, had slept around the clock. He was in his bathrobe eating breakfast when a friend telephoned that the Japs were bombing Pearl Harbor. He was so angry that he felt tempted to take his .38 and shoot Noyes and Stark.

"His fellow cryptanalyst William Friedman could only pace back and forth and mutter to himself repeatedly 'But they knew, they knew, they knew.' " And " . . . Another who had warned the United States, Kilsoo Haan, got a telephone call from Maxwell Hamilton of the State Department. He demanded that Haan's December 5 warning of a Pearl Harbor attack that weekend not be released to the press. 'If you do,' he warned, 'I can put you away for the duration.' Haan reluctantly promised to hold the report until the end of the war."

Toland ends the foregoing section with the following: "At 12:29 P.M. President Roosevelt entered the House chambers in the Capitol on the arm of his son James. There was a resounding ovation as he grasped the roster. 'Yesterday, December 7, 1941,' he began in the voice that no one who heard it would ever forget, ' — a date which will live in infamy — the United States was suddenly and deliberately attacked. . . .' "

A few hours later I spoke over the radio in the House of Representatives upholding the President's speech. I denounced the Japanese in the strongest language for their wicked attack upon the United States in the midst of peace negotiations. I pled for unity among all non-interventionists to support the administration in defeating the Japanese.

At that time I knew nothing about the war ultimatum to Japan and nothing about the coverup by Roosevelt and his war cabinet to keep information from Admiral Kimmel and General Short. Like all other members of Congress and all the American people, I was completely and totally deceived by the President of the United States.

John Toland's remarkable book goes on to say:

> By December 4, Roosevelt and a small group of advisors, including Stimson, Knox and Marshall, were faced with three options. They could announce to Japan and the world word of the approaching *Kido Butai*

(the Japanese carrier fleet); this would indubitably have forced the Japanese to turn back. Second, they could inform Kimmel and Short that Japanese carriers were northwest of Hawaii and order them to send every available long-range patrol plane to discover this force. An attack conceived in such secrecy and, once discovered, out of range of its target, *Kido Butai* would have turned back.... And the third option would accomplish this: keep Kimmel and Short and all but a select few in ignorance so that the Japanese could continue to their launching point unaware of their discovery. This would insure that the Japanese would launch their attack.

Toland sums up by writing:

What novelist could persuade a reader to accept the incredible activities during December 6 and 7 by America's military and civilian leaders? Was it to be believed that the heads of the Army and Navy could not be located on the night before Pearl Harbor? Or, that they would later testify over and over, that they couldn't remember where they were? Was it plausible that the Chief of Naval Operations, after finally being reminded that he talked to Roosevelt on the telephone that night, could not recall if they had discussed the thirteen-part message? Was it possible to imagine a President who remarked "This means war," after reading the message, not instantly summoning to the White House his Army and Navy commanders as well as his Secretaries of War and Navy? One of Knox's close friends, James G. Stahlman, wrote Admiral Kemp Tolley in 1973 that Knox told him that he, Stimson, Marshall, Stark and Harry Hopkins had spent most of the night of

December 6 at the White House with the President: All were waiting for what they knew was coming: an attack on Pearl Harbor.

The incredulities continued the following morning with Marshall insisting he did not reach his office until 11:25. Yet Stimson's military aide, Major Harrison, recently revealed in an interview that he saw the Chief of Staff in the War Secretary's office around 10:00 A.M. "I saw and talked to General Marshall: and whoever said he was out riding horses, lied, because I saw him and talked to him at that time." So had Commander McCullom and Lt. Col. John R. Deane, one of Marshall's assistant secretaries.

A massive coverup followed Pearl Harbor a few days later, according to an officer close to Marshall, when the Chief of Staff ordered a lid put on the affair. "Gentlemen," he told half a dozen officers, "this goes to the grave with us." The unnamed officer, who is still alive, had lunch on May 4, 1961, with Brig. Gen. Bonner Fellers and Dr. Charles Tansill. According to the former, the officer stated on December 7 Marshall was obviously dragging his feet regarding the warning to Short. That was why the Chief of Staff had bound certain members of his staff not to disclose the truth; and why he himself later conveniently forgot where he was on the eve of Pearl Harbor. . . .

The testimony of the Chief of Staff [George Catlett Marshall] at the various investigations does not stand up now that the prestige and glamor of his high office have gone. It was a tragedy that a man in his high position was forced to lie. So too his two trusted subordinates, Bedell Smith and Gerow. Both had refused to pass on any warning to Hawaii on December 6.

It was also a tragedy that men like Stimson, Hull and

Knox felt obliged to join in the coverup and make scapegoats of two innocent men, Kimmel and Short. Open criticism of this injustice from such prestigious naval officers as Admirals Yarnell, Richardson, King, Standley, and Halsey indicated how deep were the resentment and disgust among leading navy officers.

I have used these passages from a Pulitzer Prize-winning author, who has made the most detailed and documented study of the truth, because I did not, while I was in Congress, have any proof to expose this infamous situation. I am sure that some ardent pro-war friends of Franklin D. Roosevelt, in defending him, might say that the truth was kept from the American people because the end justifies the means. If this can be said about FDR, then it might equally be said about Hitler and Stalin.

ADDENDUM

The Betrayal of Freedom in Europe: FDR's Plan for the Communist Domination of Europe by Stalin

History records the far-reaching effects of World War II upon Europe, as well as the rest of the world. However, Franklin Roosevelt's manipulation of European affairs did not end with the cessation of armed hostilities. His plans for the postwar political realignment of the nations of Europe are fully documented — and as shocking as his maneuvering of the United States into the War.

Stalin and communism triumphed with the help of FDR, aided by Churchill, at Teheran and Yalta. Actually the sellout, or more accurately, betrayal, was prearranged by FDR.

Churchill is alleged by FDR to have acquiesced three months before Teheran in a conference between them, held in Washington, D.C., on the first two days of September 1943. Churchill's part is still vague and questionable as are whatever commitments were made to him by Roosevelt.

FDR outlined his odious plan to his close friend Bishop Francis Spellman, later Cardinal, on September 3, 1943, at the White House. Bishop Spellman took copious notes and wrote out a precise account of the statements made to him by President Roosevelt. This memorandum of two typewritten pages is contained in *The Cardinal Spellman Story* by Reverend Robert Gannon.

I knew Cardinal Spellman well. He was of the highest character and integrity. The statement is bloodcurdling in its appeasement or rather abject surrender. The memorandum is headed, "Here Are a Few Outstanding Points of the Conversation." Bishop Spellman merely reported the facts and made no comments of his own. The following are extracts, under the title "Russia" (It is important to understand that this was three months before the Teheran Conference.)

> Stalin would certainly receive Finland, the Baltic states, the eastern half of Poland and Bessarabia. Furthermore, the population of eastern Poland want to become Russian.

It is interesting to know that FDR, out of the great generosity of his heart, even agreed to give Finland to Russia without the consent of the Finns, who remained free through their own indomitable courage.

According to FDR's carefully devised plan, the world would be divided into spheres of influence:

> China gets the Far East; U.S. the Pacific; Britain and Russia get Europe and Africa. But as Britain has predominating colonial interests, it might be assumed that Russia will predominate in Europe.

In other words, more than a year and a half before the war had been won, and before any peace conferences had been held, FDR planned to give Russia not only Europe as a sphere of influence, but allow her to act as a predominating force there. The kind-hearted American president hoped

> . . . although is might be wishful thinking, that Russian intervention might not be too harsh, it is probable that the Communist regime will expand — France might eventually escape if it had a government 'a la Leon Blum. The Front Populaire would be so advanced that eventually the Communists might accept it.

President Roosevelt went on to say:

> We should not overlook the magnificent economic achievement of Russia . . . Their finances are sound. It is natural that the European countries will have to undergo tremendous changes in order to adapt to Russia. The European people (which includes France, Belgium, Holland, Denmark and Norway and of course our wartime enemies Germany and Italy) will simply have to endure the Russian domination in the hope that in ten or twenty years they will be able to live will with the Russians.

This statement of FDR's is shameful; it proposes betrayal of the freedom of France and other western European nations. It is interesting to note that Roosevelt almost always referred to the Russians, not the Communists. His statement was a travesty on Allied war aims, a mockery of the Atlantic Charter, and a repudiation of the sacrifices made by our own soldiers in Europe. It would have meant that those heroic veteran dead had died in vain.

If France had been dominated by the Communists

from Moscow, British influence in Europe would have disappeared into thin air, and, instead, a Communist Sword of Damocles, held by a wire from the Kremlin, would have been held over the heart of London and all of Britain.

It is puzzling and difficult to believe that FDR thought up this scheme for the control of western Europe all by himself. And as one who had often disagreed with him on his foreign policies, I would be inclined to believe that this abominable plan was not conceived by him alone. Roosevelt had advisors who were known to be friendly to Stalin and his regime. Among them were Lauchlin Currie, Roosevelt's executive secretary and advisor on foreign affairs, who was publicly denounced as a pro-communist and later fled; Harry Dexter White, the top representative of the Treasury Department on foreign affairs, and who was also alleged to be a pro-communist; Alger Hiss, who held a high position in the State Department and whose communist activities did not become public until much later; and possibly, Harry Hopkins, FDR's right arm, who Roosevelt had said got along with Stalin "like a house on fire." Hopkins had more influence with Stalin and also with Roosevelt than anyone else. Any one of these might well have helped in writing a plan that virtually turned over all of western Europe to Russian domination.

Some future historian, I hope, will make a thorough investigation of the story of Bishop Spellman's written memorandum. The searchlight of truth should expose its origin, protagonists and motives. It is one of the most shocking documents of the entire war, and of great historical importance. The fact that it was a written, verbatim report of a statement made by FDR to Bishop Spellman, a political friend and supporter of the President, confirms the authenticity and truth of Roosevelt's shameful postwar plans. The public may draw its own conclusions.

The real question is, who sowed the seeds in Roosevelt's mind for this odious domination of Europe by the Communists? It may never be known definitely. One thing is certain — it did not originate from Churchill, Eden, Hull, Byrnes or Sumner Welles, none of whom had any use for communism. Hull did not like General de Gaulle because of the seizure by his Free French of the islands of Saint Pierre and Miquelon, close to the southwestern coast of Newfoundland, without the knowledge or consent of our State Department.

But Cordell Hull was not vindictive. I am sure he would not have been a party in attempting to punish France to spite de Gaulle by supporting FDR's plan, and there is no evidence that Hull had any knowledge of or approved of it.

On February 15, 1971, the State Department released a number of long-withheld documents to the public. They revealed an almost incredible and vindictive hatred of de Gaulle expressed by President Franklin D. Roosevelt in 1943, at the time of the meeting of de Gaulle and Roosevelt at the Casablanca conference.

It is just as well that these bitter comments were pigeonholed for all these years, and perhaps it would have been better if they had never been released. Much of FDR's personal dislike of de Gaulle was published many years ago in his son Elliot Roosevelt's book, *As He Saw It.* Now it is the inescapable duty of an historian to add insult to injury and make the new diatribes against de Gaulle public property, although they will not make many friends for the United States among the numerous Gaullists in France.

But historically, these documents disclose the main weakness in the composition of Roosevelt's character. His personal denunciation of de Gaulle was vindictive, bad manners, and bad politics. De Gaulle was then the great hero of the Free French and of most of the French people, an acknowledged savior of France, and the almost unanimous choice of the people as the head of the provisional government. Roosevelt's attitude did not represent that of the American people, who generally admired de Gaulle for the courage of his convictions in France's darkest hours.

These tirades are typical of FDR's personality in their arrogance, vindictiveness and personal animosity. There was no reason for him to be hostile to de Gaulle, who was not a political opponent but merely a courageous and honorable Frenchman whose chief objective was the freedom and restoration of the French Republic.

In a letter to Churchill on May 8, 1943, FDR accused de Gaulle of stirring up trouble in Algiers and said, "I do not know what to do with de Gaulle; possibly you would like to make him Governor of Madagascar." Roosevelt went on to recommend the reorganizing of the French National Committee, the resistance movement de Gaulle headed. "I am sorry but it seems to me the conduct of the bride [de Gaulle] continues to be more and more aggravating." The bridegroom, according to the president, was General Henri Giraud. Roosevelt tried to bring them together. Actually he favored General Giraud over de Gaulle as chairman of the French Committee of National Liberation in exile. Roosevelt wrote, "I am inclined to think when we get into France itself we will have to regard it as a *military occupation run by British and American generals. . .* I think that this may be necessary for six months or even a year after we get into France." (Author's italics.) About 90 percent of the mayors and subordinate officials of French cities and departments could be used, Roosevelt suggested, *"but the top line of national administration must be kept in the hands of the British or American commanders-in-chief.* The old former government simply will not do." (Author's italics.)

This would mean nothing more than a foreign military autocracy or dictatorship. What a travesty on American fundamental principles and ideals of government based on freedom and self-determination of the people. This State Department release differs from Roosevelt's conversation with Bishop Spellman, four months later. Perhaps the President found that Churchill and the British were not in favor of assuming control of the government of France with the United States, so he substituted Stalin and the Communists to dominate France and the other western European nations.

Roosevelt sent the draft of the memorandum on de Gaulle to Secretary of State Hull with a note saying he thought of taking up its contents with Churchill, according to a State Department footnote to the document. Hull answered, "It is very evident that the French National Committee is basing its whole policy on the idea that when France is liberated from the

Germans, organized elements under de Gaulle will be in control."

These documents, released by the State Department, were hidden away for 32 years. They confirm Roosevelt's intense antagonism for de Gaulle and account to some extent for his odious plan to have the Russians dominate France after the war.

Again quoting from Bishop Spellman's carefully prepared written report of what FDR told him on September 3: "The Russian production is so high that American help, except for trucks, is negligible." What a misleading and incredible statement. The truth is that the bulk of the Russian factories had been destroyed by the invading German armies. The U.S. loaned Soviet Russia eleven billion dollars. Under the terms of the Lend-Lease agreement, Stalin received from the West twenty thousand aircraft, close to 400,000 trucks, twice as many trucks as the Communists had at the time of the invasion of Russia, vast quantities of leather for shoes, cloth for uniforms, hundreds of miles of barbed wire and telephone lines, railroad locomotives, automobiles, much-needed food supplies on a huge scale, and equipment for setting up new industrial plants.

These statements by FDR are so incredible and outrageous that I could not have believed them except from such an exceptional source as Francis Spellman, a trusted ally of FDR at that time. He had just returned from a six-month mission, as Roosevelt's personal representative, to Europe, Africa and South America, when he had this appalling interview with the President of the United States. The night before, he had dined at the White House with the President and

Winston Churchill. I have dealt only with the facts as stated specifically by Bishop Spellman, but I ask the reader's forebearance while I digress to conjure up a picture of FDR and Churchill, carving up the postwar world at the White House three months before the Teheran Conference. How else could FDR have spoken to Bishop spellman as he did, outlining such a terrible postwar program?

It is a mystery to me why Churchill ever consented to such ruinous terms. It is more than likely that Churchill gave only limited or lukewarm support, even though Britain was to participate in control with Russia over western Europe and Africa. In his fear and dislike of communism, Churchill was as constant as the north star. Besides, he was a realist and must have understood that FDR's postwar plans for western Europe and Africa would be disastrous to Britain and to freedom everywhere. He probably quietly and effectively undermined the whole project. Certainly the English did not want Stalin to control France, Belgium and Holland any more than they wanted Hitler to.

As for the French, they were never consulted and knew nothing about Roosevelt's shameful plan. His proposal of Russian domination for twenty years was, of course, meaningless. The Communists would have seized complete power in a few years and communized France and western Europe by force and violence. Freedom would then have been sorely stricken throughout the world.